CHURCH IN THE **INVENTIVE AGE**

CHURCH IN THE INVENTIVE AGE

DOUG PAGITT

sparkhouse press
MINNEAPOLIS

CHURCH IN THE INVENTIVE AGE

Cover art and design: Joe Vaughan
Book art and design: Joe Vaughan
Interior layout: Timothy W. Larson

Pagitt, Doug
  Church in the inventive age / Doug Pagitt.
      p. cm.
  Includes bibliographical references.
  ISBN 978–1–4514–0085–4 (alk. paper)
  1. Christianity United States. 2. Christianity and culture—United States. 3. United States Church history 21st century. I. Title.
  BR515.P34 2010
  277.3'083 dc22   2010013493

The paper used in this publication meets the minimum requirements of American National Standard for Information Sciences — Permanence of Paper for Printed Library Materials, ANSI Z329.48-1984.

Manufactured in the U.S.A.

14   13   12   11   10   1   2   3   4   5   6   7   8   9   10

"THE FUTURE IS NOT A RESULT OF CHOICES AMONG ALTERNATIVE PATHS OFFERED BY THE PRESENT, BUT A PLACE THAT IS CREATED—CREATED FIRST IN THE MIND AND WILL, CREATED NEXT IN ACTIVITY. THE FUTURE IS NOT SOME PLACE WE ARE GOING, BUT ONE WE ARE CREATING."

—JOHN SCHAAR

CONTENTS

CHAPTER 1
DEFINING OUR RELATIONSHIP

THE FUTURE IS THE SAME AS THE PAST, RIGHT
UP UNTIL THE POINT WHEN IT ISN'T.

—DOUG PAGITT

Authors are often told that a book should build a relationship between the writer and the reader. So here
we are, starting a relationship.

It's a rather strange relationship to be sure. I'm going to
do all of the talking. I don't know you but I'm going to take
my best guess so I can talk about the work you do. I'm
assuming you are a church leader of some kind—a pastor,
a ministry leader, or one of the saints among us who puts
energy into your church without pay. Maybe you're reading this book for a class or because you are on an elder
board and someone told you to read it. Maybe you've just
picked it up because it's short and you need something to
read on your flight. Maybe you've read other things I've
written or maybe you've never heard of me.

There are enough variables in this relationship that I think
we should start it with some straight talk about what this
book is and what it isn't, what I'm up to as I write and what
I hope you'll do as you read.

I am making one point in this book: The United States is in its fourth cultural age, the Inventive Age. Every cultural age has four components: how people think, what they value, a collection of aesthetic preferences, and a set of tools by which people do what they need to do. Today's churches need to decide how they want to fit into the Inventive Age and develop the components needed to live well.

I am going to throw out big ideas and move fast. This isn't a book in which I tell you what to think. It's a book in which I raise issues in order to make you think about the future of the church. I want this book to leave you with questions, to get your head spinning a bit. I want it to lead you into new conversations with the people in your church. I want to give you the language and categories to move into the future with a clear sense of who you are and where you're going.

It won't take you long to read this book. The average person reads between 200 and 250 words per minute. That means the average person could get through this book in

I'M GOING TO THROW OUT BIG IDEAS AND MOVE FAST.

about two hours. But I hope you spend far more time talking about the suggestions in the book than you do reading about them. I hope you'll spend more time putting your ideas into play than you do learning about my ideas.

As you'll see in a moment, the Inventive Age is all about collaboration and creativity. This book is my way of collaborating with you, of inspiring you to create a faith community that can thrive in our changing culture.

I can't wait to see where this relationship takes us.

CHAPTER 2
WE DON'T KNOW WHERE WE'RE
GOING, BUT WE SURE KNOW WHERE WE'VE BEEN

THE FUTURE IS ALREADY HERE, IT IS JUST
UNEVENLY DISTRIBUTED.

—WILLIAM GIBSON

We live in the midst of inescapable change. Maybe this thrills you. Maybe this scares you. Regardless, the changes happening right now in American society mean every cultural institution, every community, every individual has a choice to make: We can either be in on the change or we can be left behind.

It's only a slight exaggeration to say that everything in our lives, everything we depend on for our basic survival, was created in the last 200 years. Think about your typical day. You wake up in a bed made of materials—internal springs, polymers, anti-microbial fabrics—that didn't exist 200 years ago. You are awakened by an alarm clock that was invented in 1876 (or maybe to an iPod that was invented in 2001). You take a shower (indoor plumbing arrived in the mid-19th century); eat eggs shipped by trucks from a different part of the country, purchased at a grocery store with a credit card, and cooked over an electric stove. You drive a car to work and maybe make a few calls on your cell phone on the way.

You might live in a state that was open frontier in 1860 or in a town that was nothing but grassland in 1922. You might send your kids to a school where they read digitally printed books and use computers and watch DVDs. You might go to church on Sunday morning at 11:00 where you speak into a microphone and sing along with words projected on a screen.

The basic frameworks for communication, transportation, education, religious life, even plumbing, have been around for centuries, but the actual resources we use every day are relatively recent additions to the social landscape.

For most of human history, changes in broad social structures came occasionally and were limited in geographic scope. But in the last two centuries, cultural change has become far-reaching, constant, and increasingly rapid.

Why and how societies change is a fascinating subject, but I'm more interested in what change brings with it.

In the last 200 years, American culture has moved through three distinct ages—the *Agrarian Age*, the *Industrial Age*, and the *Information Age*—and is heavily engaged in a fourth—an era I have dubbed the *Inventive Age*. With each of these ages has come a shift in what we think, what we value, what we do, and how we do it.

Living in the Inventive Age is not optional. It's here. It is changing us. It will keep changing our culture at a breakneck speed, whether we are on board with those changes or not. If the church is going to survive, we have to do what the church has always done: figure out how to live and thrive in our culture.

CHANGE IS THE NORM, NOT THE POINT

I'm an ideas guy. I love big ideas. I get a vision for something and I'm obsessed with making it a reality.

Because of that, people think that I am always advocating for change. They hear about the church I pastor—Solomon's Porch—where we sit on couches and write our own music and create sermons as a group. They get hung up on the ways we've changed what church looks like. They hear me speak at an event and come away thinking they have to change everything they're doing—get rid of the pews, light some candles, grow facial hair—to become something other than who they are.

But that's not the kind of change to which I'm calling us.

LIVING IN THE INVENTIVE AGE IS NOT OPTIONAL.

I'm calling us to find our place in a swiftly shifting culture, to consider how we need to change what we think, what we value, what we do and how we do it. I'm calling us to be the church in the Inventive Age.

We are not called to change for change's sake. We are called to live faithfully in the time and place in which we live. Living faithfully may require us to make changes in what we do, but changing our practices is not the point. Change only matters if it's based in an understanding of why that change is needed. If it's not, the only change you'll make is to trade one set of problems for another.

When a culture changes, everything *in* the culture changes. Not all at once, but over time. The tensions we are seeing in American Christianity—declining membership in mainline churches, fractious relationships between evangelicals and mainliners, an untapped spiritual hunger among young adults—point to the discomfort change brings with it.

Your level of willingness to live with some of that discomfort will determine if this is a dangerous book or a hopeful book.

We can't pretend cultural change doesn't impact the church. It does. It always has. Every church exists in the context of a culture. Every church has inherited a culture.

Most churches meet on Sunday mornings, not because there is something sacred about 11:00 a.m. but because that was the best time for farmers to head into town for an hour. They could do their morning chores, go to church, and get home in time to eat and head back to the fields for the afternoon.[1] Those churches that still meet at 11 a.m. on Sundays, despite having not a single farmer in the congregation, are living out an inherited cultural norm.

We can't pretend churches don't bring about cultural change. They do. They always have. Again, even the most innocuous parts of our lives point to the interplay between the culture and its various institutions. Would restaurants all over the country set up Sunday brunch buffets if not for the Sunday church crowd?

Thankfully, the discomfort and the need to push through it are not new phenomena. This has been the call of the church since its birth.

YOUR CHURCH IS MORE MULTICULTURAL THAN YOU THINK

The narrative of our faith is strung together by change. We should be used to it by now.

THE REFORMERS CHANGED THE CHURCH BY REWRITING THE RULES OF AUTHORITY.

THE 1ST-CENTURY CHRISTIANS CHANGED THE
CHURCH BY INCLUDING THE GENTILES IN THE
JEWISH STORY.

THE APOSTLES CHANGED THE CHURCH BY
BELIEVING IN A RESURRECTED MESSIAH.

THE PROPHETS CHANGED THE FAITH BY TURN-
ING THE STORY OF CAPTIVITY INTO A STORY
OF REDEMPTION.

MOSES CHANGED THE FAITH BY CHASING A
PROMISE.

ABRAHAM CHANGED THE FAITH BY MAKING A
COVENANT WITH GOD.

The Gospel of Mark gives us a rather strange introduction
to Jesus. Jesus is walking alongside a lake in Galilee and
says, "The time has come. The kingdom of God is near.
Repent and believe the good news!" (Mark 1:15). For a
Jewish teacher and Messiah to be introduced walking, not
in Jerusalem, but in Galilee, meant something was changing. It's as if Mark wanted to point out that the center of
the faith was no longer the Temple but Jesus.

The New Testament tells story after story of the shift from
a faith based on the Temple and synagogue model to one
that included apostles, Gentiles, and home churches. The
Bible is clear that this process was more than-a-little
uncomfortable for the religious leaders of the day.

Still, these people understood that change comes and that
the faith compels us to move forward, not back. They faced
upheaval, doubt, even death. They faced the wondrous
task of proclaiming the kingdom of God in their day. And
that will never change.

Too often, churches stay stuck in the past and end up dying off as their lifeblood is sucked away in the name of
tradition. Just as often, churches ignore the past and move

forward with no regard for the strengths of our history. Both approaches are a mistake.

The past is not our standard. It is not the test of whether something is right or good. But it's also not an albatross we need to shuck off as quickly as possible. The past is our constant companion. It is always with us. The question is what do we do with it—return to it, let it rule, or take its best efforts with us into the future?

To answer that question, we'll start with a look at the three ages through which we have already moved and the age in which we find ourselves today.

IMPROVEMENT:
MAKES AN ORGANIZATION BETTER BY
ASSUMING THE CURRENT BUILDING BLOCKS
AND ADJUSTING THE LEAST USEFUL ELEMENTS.

INNOVATION:
USES DISRUPTIVE CHANGES TO ALTER
THE WAY THINGS ARE DONE TO
INCREASE EFFECTIVENESS.

INVENTION:
INTRODUCES AN ENTIRELY NEW MODEL THAT
IS FUNDAMENTALLY DIFFERENT AND NOT
CURRENTLY IN USE.

CHAPTER 3
CHANGE ISN'T JUST SOMETHING
YOU GET FROM A VENDING MACHINE

HISTORY CANNOT GIVE US A PROGRAM FOR
THE FUTURE, BUT IT CAN GIVE US A FULLER
UNDERSTANDING OF OURSELVES, AND OF OUR
COMMON HUMANITY, SO THAT WE CAN BET-
TER FACE THE FUTURE.

—ROBERT PENN WARREN

I was once in a small group meeting with famed organizational expert Peter Drucker. Out of everything he said, one
thought has stuck with me more than the others. He said,
"The world my parents were born into was essentially the
same as the world of Abraham and Sarah from the Bible."
He was, of course, right.

Drucker, born in Vienna in 1909, was pointing out that
the world into which his parents were born—specifically
Austria in the 19th century—operated under a social
structure that had been in place in rural areas for a millen-
nium. He contrasted that with the world into which he was
born—Austria at the dawn of the Industrial Revolution.
Just one generation earlier, the majority of human beings lived like their parents and grandparents and great-
grandparents had. They worked the land, rarely lived more
than one hundred miles from where they were born, and

knew they'd be lucky to see their 50th birthdays. Mid-19th century culture was, as Druker said, nearly identical to the culture of the ancient Israelites. Both were part of the Agrarian Age.

The Industrial Revolution of the late 1800s brought about dramatic cultural upheaval in Europe and the United States. Certainly earlier inventions like the printing press had a broad impact on society. But the printing press didn't directly change the way people fed themselves or moved from place to place or earned a living. The Industrial Revolution did.

People moved from farms to cities. Men and women who had once worked alongside each other in the fields left their families at home to work in factories. Manufactured goods became the currency of the culture.

The next cultural shift began while the Industrial Age was still booming. During the 1920s and '30s, the Information Age began to take hold, thanks in no small part to the growth of the manufacturing and shipping industries that had taken place during the Industrial Age. As people had access to books, newspapers, radios, and eventually televisions, knowledge and information became the most valuable assets of the culture.

In the same way, the Inventive Age is being born out of the Information Age. Knowledge is no longer the goal, but the means by which we accomplish new—even unimagined— goals.

THE ROLE OF THE CHURCH IS TO LIVE AS A PARTICIPANT IN THE CULTURE

Few cultural institutions have been able to move through all of these shifts with their central identity intact. The church has been a steady—though not unchanged—

presence in each age. It has remained when so many other cultural institutions have either fallen away completely or morphed so cleanly that they no longer resemble their former selves. I believe that's because the church has been both shaped by and a shaper of culture.

There are people who hate the idea that the culture impacts the church. They like to think of the church as a bastion of stability in a sea of turmoil. They want to believe that the church has somehow maintained a pristine, untouched essence even as the muck of society has swirled around it.

That's simply not the case.

This isn't an insult to the church. The church ought to place itself squarely in the midst of a culture. Everything from the kinds of buildings we call churches to the way we expect our pastors to preach, our theology to be laid out, and our furniture to be arranged is meant to communicate something to the culture in which a church functions. I think that's good news.

As American society has moved from the Agrarian Age through the Industrial Age into the Information Age and now on to the Inventive Age, the church has moved right along with it. These four ages serve not only as an overview of American history, they are a map of the landscape of American Christianity.

The Agrarian Age: Little Church on the Prairie

It might be more accurate to call the Agrarian Age the Everything-Before-the-War-of-1812 Age. As Peter Drucker pointed out, in the time between the dawn of humanity and the mid-1800s, very little changed.

Here in the United States, we have a bit of a love affair
with our agrarian past. We are an eager audience for
stories about the Wild West and the frontier. Our national
identity is built on the notion that we are rugged individu-
alists, pioneers who can conquer nature herself. On any
given day, you can still find reruns of *Little House on the
Prairie* on TV. Many parents consider it part of their civic
duty to read the Laura Ingalls books to their children.

Actually, *Little House on the Prairie* isn't a bad way to think
about the face of American culture in the Agrarian Age.
Most people lived like the Ingalls family. They built their
homes by hand. They lived in or near small towns that
were made up of a general store, a mill or grain exchange,
maybe a blacksmith or tannery, and a central building that
served as a school, a church, and a town hall. They made
a living either by working the land or by providing goods
and services to those who did.

Most people spent their entire lives surrounded by essentially the same families. They ate food grown on their land
and the land of people they knew. They made clothing out
of fabric they bought from their neighbors. They slept under blankets quilted by friends. They were present for the
births of their neighbors' children and built caskets to hold
their neighbors' dead. People were tightly tied to the land
and to each other.

While there were certainly cities in the Agrarian Age, they
were nothing like the cities Americans would see by the
end of the 19th century: In 1800, New York City had a population of 80,000. By 1900, the population had jumped to
3,000,000.

Life in the Agrarian Age was also shrouded in fear. Death
was an ever-present threat. If you and your mother sur-
vived pregnancy and childbirth, you had to worry about
pneumonia, whooping cough, scarlet fever, and
snakebites.

Once you were old enough to work the land, there were countless accidents that could rob you of your livelihood, not to mention your life. Then there was the weather. Too hot, too cold, too wet, or too dry and a year's worth of crops were gone. Tornados, fires, blizzards, floods, drought—there was no end to the ways nature could crush you.

That looming sense of fear meant that the Agrarian Age wasn't just about location. It was a mindset. There was a sense of dependence on other people, on the land, on God, on nature. This dependence was necessary for survival, yes, but it also framed the way people thought about themselves and the world around them.

You stayed close to home because you needed to trust the people around you to help you survive. You learned everything you knew from watching and listening to other people because if they'd managed to stay alive maybe you would too. There was the world you knew and the world you didn't—and would likely never—know. The fear of what lay beyond the borders of your community, the otherness of the people and places you didn't know or understand, kept you from venturing too far.

This localized, organic, almost-tribal cultural sensibility extended to the church as well. In the Agrarian Age, the church functioned under the parish model. People didn't travel to some church in another town because they preferred the music there. People belonged to the church that was closest to them. It was geography not theology that determined where you went to church. (It helped that most rural communities were ethnically mono-cultural and the people shared a similar religious background.)

The church building itself was a simple structure, built by the people in the community. It's no coincidence that many rural churches share an architectural history not with the great cathedrals of Europe but with the barns and outbuildings that marked the American landscape in the Agrarian Age.

The parish model put the pastor in the role of a shepherd of sorts—(the word *pastor* means shepherd). He—and it was always a he—was a member of the community, but he held special status as the community's moral compass. Like any good shepherd, the pastor tended his flock by walking with them, living with them, tending to them in the good and the bad, and gently guiding them in the ways of the Lord. The parishioners were the vulnerable sheep who came to church to be fed the gospel by their shepherd. In an agrarian culture, the pastor-as-shepherd metaphor held deep resonance.

AND THEN CAME THE REVOLUTION.

There are still Agrarian Age churches today—and not just in rural communities. The small storefront churches in downtown Chicago and Los Angeles and Minneapolis follow the parish model. They are non-denominational churches that draw from a small neighborhood. The pastor is deeply involved in the life of the community—she might even hold another job and serve as pastor only as a side gig. Today's parish-style churches, which often spring up as a response to the fears that come with living in a run-down city neighborhood or a dying rural farm town, continue to provide a sense of community in places where life remains uncertain.

Between diseases, natural disasters, and the sheer effort involved in staying alive, it's amazing human beings managed to survive the Agrarian Age. Yet for thousands of years, cultures all over the world and right here in the United States were defined by this rural, localized, communal sensibility.

And then came the revolution.

The Industrial Age: The Captains of Christianity

While Great Britain and the rest of Europe went through their own Industrial Revolution in the late 18th century, the United States held on to its agrarian identity a bit longer. But the Embargo Act of 1807, which limited what could be imported from Europe, and the War of 1812 led to this country becoming—from an economic standpoint at least—completely self-reliant. That meant building the infrastructure to manufacture and transport the goods necessary to support a growing nation.

Rail lines were laid and roads built and lights turned on and phone calls recorded. The social structure of the nation shifted from the fields to the streets.

As transportation became more available, it became easier—not to mention less life-threatening—for rural people to move into the city in search of a better life for themselves and their families. There were still plenty of farms and wide-open spaces, but the population center was clearly shifting.

The city was where the jobs were. There was a fortune to be had and it didn't take long for tales of the hometown boy turned factory foreman to make their way back to the farm.

The population migration wasn't only the result of f armers moving into town. Much of the rise in population was due to the arrival of immigrants. As these groups came across the ocean and settled into the cities, they created their own neighborhoods and communities. For the first time in American history, people from vastly different parts of the world lived side-by-side.

The population was both expanding in size and compress-
ing in area. By the end of the 19th century, a person in
New York City lived within walking distance of 2 million
people. That brought with it a whole new set of challenges.
The rush to build housing led to shoddy work and dangerous tenement buildings. Disease spread rapidly in the
close quarters of the city.

If you think air pollution is a 20th-century problem, think
again. Horses were still the main mode of transportation,
even in the city. But the methane created by their dung
made the city air toxic—lung disease was one of the biggest health threats of the era. There was great hope that
with the arrival of the automobile the air would be cleaner
and people would once again breath easier.

At the heart of the Industrial Revolution was the factory.
Just as farming defined the Agrarian Age, manufacturing
defined its successor. It was the factory—and the jobs it
provided—that drew people to the city. It was the factory
that made the rivets and the gears and the engines that
built the nation. It was the factory that produced the newspapers and the radios that spread news from the cities to
other parts of the country for the first time. And it was the
captains of industry—men with names like Carnegie and
Rockefeller—who changed the face of America.

They did it by shifting the cultural values of the Agrarian
Age to new ways of thinking and doing and being. Dependence was replaced by domination—there was no need to
fear nature when human ingenuity could give you wells
and pipes and tractors and medicine and refrigeration to
fight her off.

That's how the Industrial Age introduced Americans to the
concept of repeatability. Once it became possible to put a
furnace in a house and give medicine to a sick child, there
was a national sense of urgency to get new goods and ser-

vices to as many people as possible as quickly as possible. The emphasis was on efficiently repeating a process until the need was met.

It seemed as though every year brought with it a life-changing innovation: the telegraph, the telephone, the radio, the automobile, the airplane. Thomas Edison, the poster boy for the Industrial Age, famously said, "Be courageous. I have seen many depressions in business. Always America has emerged from these stronger and more prosperous. Be brave as your fathers before you. Have faith! Go forward!" There was a growing confidence among Americans that anything was possible in this great nation.

THE EMPHASIS WAS ON EFFICIENTLY REPEATING A PROCESS UNTIL THE NEED WAS MET.

The shift in cultural values changed the church as well. The small parish model still worked in the dwindling rural communities, but churches in the city functioned in a whole new way. People needed places to gather, so churches popped up in the middle of all those factories. The immigrant populations wanted their own churches, with services in their native languages.

So there was a German church and an Irish church and an Italian church and an English church, often within blocks of each other. Some were even built by those same captains of industry and looked very much like factories—fortresses with smokestack-like steeples and red brick facades.

It wasn't just the European churches that were booming in the United States. Whole new religions appeared. This period saw the birth of Mormonism, Christian Science, and a host of now-defunct, distinctly American religions and religious orders.

As these churches grew, so did the desire for their congregations to replicate those in the old country. So the Industrial Age gave rise to the modern-day denominational system. There was an effort to codify spiritual teaching to make sure everyone could tell the difference between a Lutheran church and a Methodist church and a Presbyterian church.

The urban environment created a new kind of denominational competition. In the Agrarian Age, churches were set apart by language and location. Now there were ten churches representing ten denominations all on the same street. This created stress for pastors, who now had to not only shepherd a flock but had to actively convert people from other expressions of Christianity—not to mention protect their own flocks from being recruited.

The role of the pastor was to teach the congregation the theology of the denomination and to make it compelling enough that people would come back for more. They were educated in denominational seminaries where they learned the polity and doctrine that made their version of Christianity unique. The pastor's job was, like a factory foreman, to build Lutherans (or Methodists or Episcopalians), to make sure the denominational distinctives were carried on. They were building a denominational brand.

The Industrial Age church is alive and well today. The strength of the denominational system allows for the kind of international, cooperative efforts we saw after the earthquake in Haiti and in the ongoing human rights challenges in African nations. Denominations allow for partnerships across cultures as churches around the world address the particular needs of their churches with the resources of the denomination at their disposal.

America was built in the Industrial Age. There is not a city in the United States that doesn't bear the marks of the great railroads and factories and innovations of the 19th century. While the coming Information Age would change so much about culture, it did so on the shoulders of the Industrial Age.

 The Information Age: It's What You Know

The shift from the Industrial Age to the Information Age was not nearly as well-defined as the shift out of the Agrarian Age. It could be argued that the Industrial Age never really ended. In the sense that we still make things, I suppose that's true. But the values of the culture, the sense of who we are, what we do, and how we do it have changed dramatically.

It didn't take long for the urban centers to become so crowded that people began to move from the center of a city to its edges. This migration led to a whole new designation of location—the "sub"-urban city. In the 1940s, soldiers returning from World War II were given money through the new GI Bill to, among other things, help them buy homes or land. And they did. Young families bought up tract houses on former farmland and turned these fields into communities.

Unlike the enclaves of the city, suburban neighborhoods tended to be relatively cross-cultural compared to the distinct "sub towns" of the city. With the painful exception of Jewish people and African Americans, who were often turned away from banks and pushed out of neighborhoods, the suburbs were made of up people from all kinds of backgrounds. As immigrant families had children and grandchildren, the family's identity became less connected to its homeland and more generally Americanized.

By the year 2000, nearly half of the American population lived in the suburbs.

At the center of these suburbs were schools. Like the old parish church, the school served as the communal gathering place for the neighborhood. School buildings popped up like newly planted trees in the burgeoning housing developments and in the urban centers.

This organizational pattern was due in large part to the increased value of education. Education was the way to get ahead, to get out of the factory and forge a better life. Literacy rates rose. Teachers were respected leaders in their communities. The first high schools opened up. College became a real option for an increasing number of high school graduates.

The culture no longer valued what you made. It valued what you knew. The more you knew, the more power you had.

There was a drive to understand, to dig in, to learn and discover and dissect—whether it was frogs in a junior high science class or atoms in a physics laboratory. The Industrial Age made it possible to send mass-produced schoolbooks all over the country. For the first time, students across the United States could learn from books that included color photographs of other countries, other cultures. The world was knowable and Americans wanted to know it all.

The rise in literacy and the availability of books made for a rash of nationally known experts in medicine, parenting, science, even exercise. For the first time, authors became household names, their words used to make an argument, settle a bet, inspire a change, feed a child.

Then there was television. If the Information Age has an icon, it's the television set. Because of its immediacy, it quickly became the primary source of news and information. Something happening on the other side of the country, the other side of the planet, even on the moon, was now just a telecast away.

This craving for knowledge, for understanding, worked its way into the church as well. While Sunday school had been around for generations, the Information Age marked the birth of the "education wing" on the church building. Churches either added large classrooms to their Industrial Age buildings or bought land and built churches that included gymnasiums, classrooms, and kitchens, just like the school buildings around them.

The belief that the educational model was the best way to pass the faith on to the next generation translated into camps, Vacation Bible School, curricula, and training conferences for Sunday school teachers. It grew to include adult education classes in the fellowship hall and large, interdenominational crusades where Christians gathered to learn more about their faith.

Churches became learning centers. There were parenting classes and marriage seminars, women's Bible studies and men's devotions, youth groups and preschools. There were "4 Spiritual Laws" and "Steps to Peace with God." While your denomination still mattered, the real test of a church was what you learned there. If you weren't learning anything, you left. Non-denominational churches exploded onto the scene, focusing on the soundness of their teaching techniques and the correctness of their content, not their ties to some nation-wide collective.

The Information Age gave us the pastor as teacher and eventually pastor as CEO. His sermon topic was advertised on a sign outside the church—it was the message, the lesson for the day that was important. A church was judged by the power of the pastor's teaching, his ability to leave the members of his congregation nodding their heads and taking notes like good students. The CEO pastor—who gained his position by earning an advanced degree in a seminary and passing the rigors of an ordination process that ensured he knew what he needed to know—was expected to run an organization that would bring in more people and keep the church growing.

It was the perfect birthing place for the evangelical church in America. If there was a hunger for knowledge, a longing to dig in and dissect and understand, then the populace was wide open to hearing the gospel. But if people wanted understanding, wanted knowledge, then the church needed to codify its teaching. So the gospel became not a long, messy series of stories about God made flesh, but a lesson you could learn in a tract about steps and spiritual laws, or in a didactic sermon.

By the end of the 20th century, churches borrowed as much from shopping malls as they did schools. Many sanctuaries looked like movie theaters and Sunday schools looked like Disney World. The idea was to draw people in so they could be taught the gospel, so they could gain the knowledge needed to keep their faith vibrant and alive. If it took putting in a coffee shop and a bookstore and an information booth to get people interested in church, then that's what we gave them. That was the call of the Information Age.

In churches all over the country, the Information Age is thriving. Mega-churches continue to grow and celebrity pastors continue to write books and sell out seminars so they can teach us about faith, about leadership, about marriage or church or the Bible. Clearly, the Information Age is not over.

But a new age is dawning.

BUT A NEW AGE IS DAWNING . . .

CHAPTER 4
TWEETS FROM SPACE MATTER
TO YOUR CHURCH

CHANGE IS THE ESSENCE OF LIFE. BE WILLING
TO SURRENDER WHAT YOU ARE FOR WHAT
YOU COULD BECOME.

—UNKNOWN

It's clear that something is shifting. The first time I used the Internet, I imagine my reaction was a bit like that of the early pioneers seeing a train traverse the prairie for the first time. Something I never even knew I wanted suddenly became indispensable. It was a moment when I was reminded that the future is all about possibility.

THE INVENTIVE AGE: CREATING OUR FUTURE

This is the Inventive Age. It's an age when we have no idea what's coming next or where it will come from—and it's thrilling. Much of what we knew for certain fifteen, even ten years ago—that you needed a cable coming into your house to make phone calls, that a car could only run on gas, that once you started wearing glasses you had to wear them for life—has been turned upside down.

27

Right now, we live in a world filled with ideas and tools and discoveries we couldn't have imagined 20 years ago. There is bioengineered corn growing in the African desert. You can carry a library's worth of books in your hand and your entire CD collection in your pocket. Scientists can create entirely new materials at the sub-atomic level. You can get a college degree from your living room. There are people living in a space station! What's more, I can talk to them through my Twitter account!!

In 1963 the U.S. Patent and Trademark Office processed 90,982 applications. In 2008 it processed 485,312. While the U.S. population doubled in that time, patent applications have increased more than five times.

But the Inventive Age isn't solely about inventions any more that the Agrarian Age was solely about farming. As in the previous ages, the Inventive Age is marked by changes in the way we think, what we value, what we do, and how we do it.

I BET YOU DIDN'T SEE THIS COMING

When I was in 7th grade, my social studies teacher, Mr. Bancroft, told my class that most of us would spend our lives in careers that did not yet exist. I don't know about the rest of those kids, but I certainly couldn't have said I would one day start a business as social media consultant. There was no such thing as social media in 1978 much less people who helped other people figure out how to make the most of it.

Mr. Bancroft was on to something. He knew we were moving into an age when the future would be just a few steps ahead of us. He understood the tremendous change ahead and taught us that we needed to keep our eyes peeled for how we would fit into what wasn't yet there. He recognized that we were moving into a culture of creativity.

In every sphere of society—the hard sciences, social sciences, art, sports, music, health, technology, economics, transportation, communication—there is a level of creativity that surpasses even the Industrial Age for its impact on the culture.

That creativity has altered the way we think about ourselves. Children, young adults, and even older folks no longer wonder what they will be when they grow up. Now we ask, "What do I want to do with my life? How do I want to spend my time? What can I contribute?" These aren't questions about vocation, they are questions about impact, about meaning. We sense that there is no end to the options and that the future is ours to make.

Anousheh Ansari grew up in Tehran. She eventually moved to the United States with her family and studied electrical engineering and computer science. After trying a few small business ventures, she and her husband made a fortune in the telecom industry. In 2006, she paid $20 million for a seat on a Soyuz space mission to the space station, becoming the first Muslim woman in space. In an interview with NPR she said, "I look at my trip and how many lives

WE SENSE THAT THERE IS NO END TO THE OPTIONS AND THAT THE FUTURE IS OURS TO MAKE.

it has touched and how much hope it has brought to a lot of young girls around the world. I would even say that alone was worth it. And it was at a time that people in Iran were subject to a lot of negative publicity, negative news, and just something that was positive, something that had

the word Iran in it and next to it was something positive
brought them joy. I think that that was definitely worth it."[1]
At the heart of creativity is a kind of optimism that echoes
the Industrial Age belief that human beings can do what-
ever they set out to do. But this time around, the power to
turn that belief into action is not in the hands of the few,
those captains of industry. (Of course in Ansari's case it
didn't hurt that she had a spare $20 million bucks.) Now it
is in the hands of the individual. Consider that every two
months there is more original content put up on YouTube
than if ABC, NBC, and CBS had showed original content 24

THE INVENTIVE AGE IS ONE IN WHICH INCLUSION, PARTICIPATION, COLLAB- ORATION, AND BEAUTY ARE ESSENTIAL VALUES.

hours a day, 7 days a week, 365 days a year since 1948 (a
statistic—one that will already be out-of-date by the time
you read this—I discovered from user-created content on
YouTube).[2]

The Inventive Age is one in which inclusion, participation, collaboration, and beauty are essential values. The
values of the previous ages still exist, but in different,
even subservient, roles. Knowledge is important, but only
as a means to discovering something else. Repeatability
matters but only as it relates to advancing an idea. Survival, however, is barely on the radar of most Americans;
where nature was once a major threat, it is now something we have tamed and used and manipulated so heav-

ily that there are cultural movements designed to save it. Not long ago, humanity feared the earth. Now we fear *for* the earth.

This is the age of Pandora, where I tell an online radio station what to play. It is the age of the App Store, where a major corporation hands control over to an open-source network of ordinary people. It is the age of Wikipedia, where anyone can decide what a word or concept or cultural touchstone means. It is the age when a bunch of college kids create a social network and six years later it has more than 250 million users. (If it were a country, Facebook would be the 4th largest in the world.)[3]

It is the age of ownership and customization and user-created content.

SO WHAT ARE YOU GOING TO DO ABOUT THAT?

The impetus behind all of this personalization is not narcissism. It's the longing to attach meaning to experiences. People in the Inventive Age are looking for a sense of ownership, not of things or even ideas, but of our lives. We are keenly aware of our global community and how interconnected our lives are with the lives of people all over the world. That sense of global community can be overwhelming. We want both to create our own place in that community and to contribute to its vitality. We don't want to simply use resources created by and controlled by others. Like Anousheh Ansari, we want to be participants in the amazing future we see in front of us.

As a result, there is a shift in the seat of authority. It isn't in the wisdom of the village leaders or the deep pockets of the factory owners or the knowledge of the corporate executives. Authority is found in the way our experiences come together and create reality. It is found in relationships. We tend to be suspicious of objectivity, uncertain if it is possible or even desirable. Instead, we give great credence to authenticity, to context. Authority—as much as anything else in the Inventive Age—is user generated.

The implications for the church are just beginning to emerge. In the last 10 years or so, the values of the Inventive Age—the drive to create, the search for meaning, the sense of ownership, the open-source mentality that pushes the Inventive Age ever-faster into the future—have scattered across the landscape of American Christianity like seeds in the wind.

How they will take root remains to be seen. What is clear is that just as the previous ages created the norms of the church in their day, so it will be in the Inventive Age. And just as church leaders in those ages asked difficult questions about change, so it will be up to you to decide how you will be the church in this age.

The most obvious shift is the move toward smaller churches that facilitate connection. While the Information Age church gave us small groups as a means for developing deeper knowledge, the small communities of the Inventive Age come from a longing to find meaning through shared, self-generated experiences, to live out the faith in the company of a small community of friends.

We are also seeing churches take on the role of cooperative studio space. The drive for creativity and participation draws people of the Inventive Age to faith communities in which they have a presence, in which their hopes and dreams and passions can be expressed. So, like an artist's co-op, the church becomes a place in which people of faith come to practice and hone their spiritual lives.

Inventive Age churches are centered not on location, denomination, or information, but on participation. The days of people walking into a church, sitting down, taking notes, having coffee, then heading home will come to an end as people of the Inventive Age increasingly expect the customization and ownership they find in every other part of their lives to be central to their church experiences as well. Participation will become the norm.

There is also recognition that the ways in which we experience church are contextual. Our global perspective has shown us that the Christian faith takes on other forms and other functions in other parts of the world. That understanding intrigues us and moves us to consider the ways in which our American expressions of faith are bound to our American culture.

The role of the pastor is changing as well. The ability to teach and preach and lead is taking a back seat to the pastor's capacity to create and facilitate open-source faith experiences for the people of the church.

It's far too early to know where all of this will lead. To be sure, the Inventive Age will have its share of mistaken notions, questionable practices, and bad ideas. But right now, at the dawning of a new age, it feels like a beautiful revolution.

THE ABILITY TO TEACH AND PREACH AND LEAD IS TAKING A BACKSEAT TO THE PASTOR'S CAPACITY TO CREATE AND FACILITATE OPEN-SOURCE FAITH EXPERIENCES FOR THE PEOPLE OF THE CHURCH.

LOCATION	RURAL	URBAN	SUBURBAN	GLOBAL
OUTLOOK	DEPENDENCE	DOMINANCE	DISSECTION	DISCOVERY
SUCCESS	SURVIVAL	REPEATABILITY	EXPERTISE	CREATIVITY
RELATIONSHIPS	SINGLE CULTURE	SIDE-BY-SIDE	UBIQUITOUS	PLURALISTIC
CHURCH	PARISH	DENOMINATIONS	LEARNING CENTER	CO-OP
CHURCH LEADER	SHEPHERD	PREACHER	TEACHER	FACILITATOR

CHAPTER 5
CULTURE HAS NOTHING
TO DO WITH THE BALLET

THE IDEA OF A SINGLE CIVILIZATION FOR
EVERYONE, IMPLICIT IN THE CULT OF
PROGRESS AND TECHNIQUE, IMPOVERISHES
AND MUTILATES US.

—OCTAVIO PAZ

I was an anthropology major in college. I chose anthropology not because I wanted to dig up bones but because I have always been fascinated by human beings and the cultures we create. In the geeky world of anthropology, we define a culture as "the totality of socially transmitted behavior patterns, arts, beliefs, institutions, and all other products of human work and thought." In other words, culture is defined by what we think, what we value, what we do, and how we do it.

We can see these four cultural markers in every era and every society in recorded history. They are what help us categorize people and epochs. When we talk about prehistoric tribes, ancient empires, medieval kingdoms, and primitive societies, we know which people and countries and cultures belong where based on their thought and language, their value system and religious practices, their art and architecture and music, their tools and resources.

But these cultural markers help us do more than catalogue other people and other eras. They are a way of making sense of the age in which we live. As we move from the Information Age to the Inventive Age, the interplay between these four markers helps us make sense of the changes taking place and their implications for the church.

Culture is a kind of language. And as with any language, once we become fluent in our culture, we stop thinking about it. It's much easier to see these markers in action in a culture that is not our own. They are what make other groups of people different from us—and we tend to pay attention differences.

If a friend from Guatemala comes to visit me in Minnesota in January, he will notice that in this culture we don't hesitate to walk our dogs when it's 10 degrees outside. He will notice that we value stoicism and don't have much time for complainers. He will notice that we don't cancel school when we get 5 inches of snow, that we don't mind wearing several layers of clothing even if they make us look ridiculous, and that we have several different kinds of shovels to handle various kinds of snow. I barely notice any of this.

Like language, our cultural acquisition starts at birth— if not before. Cultural norms determine the kind of pregnancy our mothers go through, the kind of birth experience we have. Once we arrive, we are thrust into a sea of cultural assumptions that show up in the kind of bed we sleep in, the kind of food we are given, the kind of medical care we receive.

Then there's the behavioral part of cultural absorption. We smile and someone smiles back and a normative pattern develops. We are taught to hold a pencil or eat with a fork and we step deeper into our culture's assumptions. We learn what to think, what to value, what to do, and how to do it.

IN EVERY AGE, THE CHURCH
HAS FOUND A WAY TO MAKE SENSE

Our churches are affected by these cultural shifts because they are cultural institutions. That's a distasteful idea for some Christians. For the last ten years, I've been involved in an ongoing conversation with a pastor friend of mine who suggests that Christianity should never be hyphenated. He told me, "Anytime you have a hyphenated Christianity you negate the Christianity." He doesn't think we should make a distinction between Korean-Christians or Pakistani-Christians or First-Century-Christians. They should be Christians *in* those times and places, not *of* them. The call to be Christian is sufficient. In his view, the hyphens only serve to water down the true faith.

His desire for a culturally neutral faith is simply not feasible. We can't use language or meet at a particular time or wear clothes or know where to sit at a table without bumping into cultural norms. The church, like every other part of a culture, is always deciding what cultural norms to follow and what cultural norms to create.

The songs we sing, the way we talk about the Bible, the role of women and children and the elderly, the arrangement of our furniture, the time we meet, the food we share—these are expressions of a culture.

We live quite contentedly in the midst of these assumptions until they are challenged. Then we get passionate. We get defensive. We get hardnosed. And sometimes we get shoved into uncomfortable places that challenge us and make us rethink our assumptions to the point that we can no longer hold on to them.

And that's good. Culture is dynamic. When we add a regional accent or phrase to the language, we are changing the culture. When we add a new ingredient to grandma's meatloaf, we are changing the culture. When we refuse

WHEN ENOUGH OF THESE TWEAKS IN WHAT PEOPLE THINK, VALUE, DO, AND USE TAKE HOLD, THE ENTIRE CULTURE SHIFTS.

to walk our dogs in sub-zero temperatures, we are changing the culture. When we realize an assumption no longer holds meaning for us and we move toward a new assumption, we are changing the culture. This has been true through all of human history. When enough of these tweaks in what people think, value, do, and use take hold, the entire culture shifts from one age to the next.

THE COMPONENTS OF CULTURE

I find it helpful to think of the four cultural components as four parts of one body. The way people within a particular culture think and use language is like the head. The values of a culture are its heart. The aesthetics of a culture—the kinds of artifacts it creates—are the gut. And the tools a culture uses and develops are its hands. (This act is itself an expression of my culture. In 1st-century Mesopotamia, the heart was the place of knowing, not feeling. And the very idea of breaking the body into parts would be non-sensical to many cultures around the world today.)

Like the body parts I'm using to represent them, none of these components creates or represents a culture on its own—all four are always present. But for the purposes of this book, I will discuss them separately.

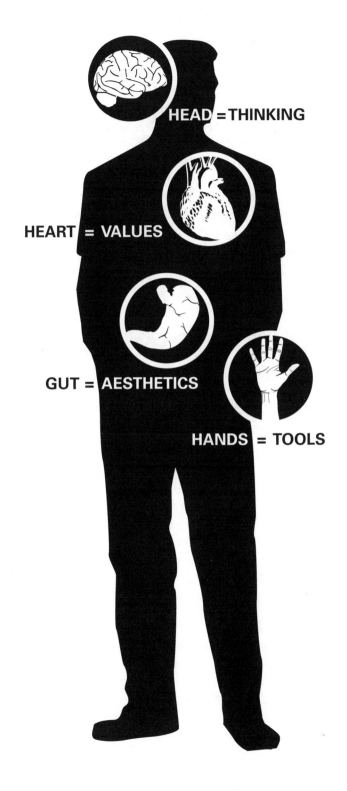

HEAD = THINKING

HEART = VALUES

GUT = AESTHETICS

HANDS = TOOLS

THE HEAD

In February of 2010, Boa Sr, a woman in her 80s, died. Her death was lamented around the world. That's because Boa Sr was the last person fluent in the Bo language of the Andaman Islands in the Bay of Bengal. When she died, a 65,000-year-old culture died with her. One linguist said, "Her loss is not just the loss of the Great Andamanese community, it is a loss of several disciplines of studies put together, including anthropology, linguistics, history, psychology, and biology. To me, Boa Sr epitomized a totality of humanity in all its hues and with a richness that is not to be found anywhere else."[1]

Even though there are artifacts from the Boa Sr culture, without language, there is no longer a way to truly uncover her culture's understanding of the world.

In an interview with NPR, one of the last living speakers of Inupiaq, the language of the Inupiat Eskimos of Alaska, said, "Without our language, our culture dies, you know. Like when we speak of food and what we hunt and how we hunt and where we hunt, most of our lands that I know is in Inupiaq names."[2]

The language-learning software company Rosetta Stone has developed an endangered language program in an effort to save languages like Inupiaq. In doing so, they have seen how language and culture create one another. The software uses images to teach language, but the company has found that images are not universal. For example, in creating the software for the Inupiaq language, they discovered that there is no Inupiaq word for "cheese" because the Inupiats don't have cheese—the image of a hunk of cheddar is meaningless. Instead, the program teaches the word for "whale blubber."[3]

Each of the four ages discussed in the previous chapters

had its own way of thinking about the world. For the people of the Agrarian Age, the world was small, rural, local, and deadly. Their language reflected the realities of their daily lives.

The same was true in the Industrial and Information Ages. The belief that human beings could accomplish anything they set out to do brought about the language of manufacturing and making and building—people talked about being a cog in a wheel or a piece of the whole. Words we use every day—cereal, pasta, kosher, marathon, bridge, aspirin, claustrophobia—came into the English lexicon along with the discoveries that necessitated them.

Today we talk about being wired, about things being high-tech or low-tech. We say we don't have the bandwidth to think about a new idea or that we have to google something to learn more about it.

Language is a key for unlocking the worldview of a culture. The pastoral language of the Agrarian Age underscores that culture's sense of interdependence and looming danger. It points to what people of that age knew and valued and understood. In the Inventive Age, the language of potential, of possibility, of creativity and organic growth pops up in our conversations, in our advertising, in our sense of what life is about and how we are to live it.

THE HEART

There's a question in medical ethics that is helpful in our discussion as well: When is a person truly dead? Is it when the heart gives out or when the brain stops working? And for people facing the death of a loved one, this is a heartbreaking and confusing distinction. Where is the source of life located? How do you know when it's gone for good?

The heart and the brain are connected in such a way that one can't survive long without the other. The same is true for the heart and head components of a culture.

The values of a culture—what it deems important, necessary, noble, and non-negotiable—are so tightly bound up with a culture's worldview that it's nearly impossible to determine which comes first.

My friend Victor often travels to his company's India branch to conduct group training sessions. After a few of these sessions, he noticed that no one ever asked questions during the training. Instead, they would seek him out after the sessions for private conversations.

Victor couldn't figure out why these employees would nod their heads in understanding during the session and then come to him with questions and concerns. Finally, he asked one of the employees why they hadn't asked for clarification during the training. The person explained that they would never insult him by questioning his presentation in front of others, that it would violate their sense of propriety to suggest he had been anything but clear.

Deference to authority is a central piece of Indian culture. It reflects the strong sense of personal and professional hierarchy that flows throughout Indian culture. So which came first—the value of deference or the belief that there are people to whom deference is owed? Who knows? But both the head component and the heart component of this practice tell us something about Indian culture.

The values of a culture often sneak up on us. It's easy to find the differences in language and even the differences in understanding—it's fairly obvious why the Inupiat Eskimos don't have a word for cheese. But values? Those don't show up until we collide with them.

THE VALUES OF A
CULTURE—WHAT IT
DEEMS IMPORTANT,
NECESSARY, NOBLE,
AND NON-NEGOTIABLE—
ARE SO TIGHTLY BOUND
UP WITH A CULTURE'S
WORLDVIEW THAT IT'S
NEARLY IMPOSSIBLE
TO DETERMINE WHICH
COMES FIRST.

We tend to believe values are universal. We think of them as essential to our humanity. They run the gamut from the deeply meaningful to the mundane. We have values about how we mange time, what size families ought to be, how we share resources, and how we greet our friends. We don't understand why someone wouldn't want to be on time, why anyone would have eight kids, why our tax dollars should pay for other people's health problems, why anyone would greet their friends with anything but a hug and a kiss on the cheek. Our values define our sense of normal.

That's why we have such a hard time with cultures in which girls are not allowed to go to school or extended families live together in the same small house. Honor killings, female circumcision, selling children—these cultural values seem horrifying to us because they are in such extreme conflict to the values of our culture.

Values are so culturally bound that we often struggle to define our own values, much less recognize those of other cultures. We just know what we think is right and what we think is wrong. When cultural shifts come along, the values shift as well. And for many of us, that is the single most difficult part of change. We can't envision a culture in which the values differ from those we know and assume to be right.

But there was a time in this country when it was culturally acceptable for one person to own another person. There was a time women were not allowed to vote. There was a time when it was illegal for people of different races to marry. The changes that led to the end of those values seem so right to us today. But they happened slowly and with great difficulty. A culture simply doesn't change its values easily.

THE GUT

The connection between the stomach, or gut, and aesthetics—what I think of as the "products" of a culture—comes from my belief in the "gut instinct." Aesthetics are highly personal. What you find lovely or useful or tasty might be ugly and pointless and disgusting to someone else. You can try to explain why it appeals to you, but it doesn't change the other person's response. Our guts tell us what we like.

Cultures have a gut-level aesthetic of their own. Here in the United States, we have particular ideas about what food should taste like, how people should smell, which clothes and buildings are "classic" and which are "tacky." Everything we create within our culture has a uniquely American feel to it.

We have distinctly American music and literature and television and movies, a distinctly American volume when we speak, a distinctly American sense of personal space. If you've ever traveled outside of the United States, you no doubt realized very quickly that our aesthetics are not necessarily shared by the rest of the world.

A culture's aesthetics aren't made up of a singular element. They are not limited to food or music or architecture. They are expressions and outcroppings of the worldview and values of the culture. That's why aesthetics shift along with a culture. As the worldview and values change, the aesthetics change with them.

American architecture offers a ready example. Think about the buildings that were prevalent in the Agrarian Age. Most of them were built by the people who lived in them and used them. They were simple, unadorned, and meant primarily to keep the weather and the wildlife at bay. They reflected the need for security and safety that permeated the culture.

By the Industrial Age, the architectural aesthetic changed along with the worldview and values of the culture. Think about the mansions built by the Rockefellers, the Vanderbilts, the Carnegies—buildings that still stand today and serve to remind us of this country's illustrious past. Those buildings were meant to inspire the common man to work harder, build faster, and make his own fortune. They were symbols of the values of the age.

The Information Age saw the emergence of the single-family home with a yard and a garage and a fence. A three-bedroom house wasn't intended to shelter three generations of family. It wasn't meant to impress others. It was built as a refuge from the demands of the city, the pressures of work. It was a place where the family could regroup and have meals together in their eat-in kitchen and invite friends over for a meal in the dining room. For the first time, it wasn't just mansions that had public and private spaces. Now everyone could have a mini-mansion of their very own.

The big thing in Inventive Age architecture is to go green. Environmental sustainability is the hallmark of the new American home. The more green the technology or technique, the better. We want our houses to tread lightly on the earth.

We also want them to "flow"—we don't want separate rooms for separate tasks. We want great rooms and open kitchens and places for people to gather. We want to rehab old houses and bring them back to life. We want to live near other people and invest in close-knit neighborhoods. The values of the Inventive Age are changing the way we set up house.

Whether it's the houses or the music or the food or the sense of personal space, the aesthetics of a culture are the artifacts it leaves behind as it makes the slow but certain shift toward change.

THE HANDS

The hands are an odd part of the human body. They are relatively simple appendages made of bone and nerves and muscle — compare them to the eyes, for example, which are made up of something like 40 different systems all working together. But even with their no-frills structure, hands are the ultimate multitaskers.

Think about everything your hand can do. It can pinch a baby's cheek, open a pickle jar, throw a ball, rub out a smudge, type an e-mail, and hold a pencil. It can snap, clutch, caress, grab, pick, pull, tap, smash, smooth, rumple, turn, twist, and slap. Doctors can replace your heart with a machine, but so far, science has been unable to come up with a machine that can do everything the human hand can do.

That's why hands are the perfect symbol for the tools of a culture.

Archeologists often look at the tools of a culture to figure out what kind of work was important to a group of people — how did they eat, find shelter, stay warm, stay safe? But the tools of a culture, while often simple and straightforward, also serve the dual purpose of reflecting a culture's values and reshaping them.

The Amish are keenly aware of the power of tools. They limit the scope of the tools they use because they know that tools change a culture. So while the Amish drive, they choose horses and buggies over cars. They have light in their homes, but it comes from oil lamps not light bulbs. The choice of tools is made based on how that tool will impact the community.

For the Amish, contact with "outsiders" is problematic. So they limit their tools to those they can create and repair within their community. They reject tools like radios and televisions that would bring the outside world into theirs. Tools that strengthen the community are welcome, those that might compromise the community are not.

Tools, like hands, are capable of far more than their simple forms suggest.

While the worldview, values, and aesthetics of a culture can take decades—even centuries—to shift, the tools of a culture change rapidly. And while they often change to meet the needs of a culture, just as often, they create need where none existed.

Take bookshelves for example. In the 1930s, the book market was slowing down. Several major publishing companies joined together to hire a public relations strategist to help them sell more books. Among his ideas was to have architects, contractors, and decorators put bookshelves in homes. The idea was that if there were bookshelves, there would soon be books.[4]

It worked. The mid-20th century was the zenith of book sales. So which came first: the bookshelves or the books they held? Did the increased number of books in a household bring about the Information Age or were they a reflection of that age's belief in the value of knowledge? The answer is, I think, both.

Consider, too, that I had only a vague recollection of the bookshelf story when I started working on this chapter. I sent out a message on Twitter—which then fed my Facebook page and blog—and within an hour I had people on all three networks sending me links to the full story. The tool of the Internet has changed the way I think about information. Nothing is unknowable because I have the force of collective knowledge at my fingertips. I have full confidence that someone in my community can help me find what I need.

IN SOME CASES, INVENTION IS THE MOTHER OF NECESSITY.

Once a tool changes our sense of what's possible, it becomes inconceivable to hold on to the old way of thinking or understanding or being. Lately I've found myself saying, "I'm not sure *where* I know that. Maybe in my head. Maybe in my computer. Maybe online. But I am fairly sure I know it somewhere." I no longer think of my brain as the source of my knowledge. Information is everywhere and I can access it in any number of ways.

In some cases, tools shift our values so completely that they change our sense of morality. When we know that we can save millions of children's lives with a polio vaccine, it becomes immoral not to do so.

In some cases, invention is the mother of necessity.

The tools of a culture tell us about that culture's worldview, its values, its aesthetics. And like those other components, tools are neither good nor bad, just different.

I heard of an Afghani man who said to a Western journalist, "You know what the problem is with you Westerners when you come to a country like this? It is this: one-third of the world eats with a fork and knife, like you. One-third eats with sticks, like the Chinese. And one-third eats with their hands, like me. And the thing you Westerners fail to realize is that none is more civilized than the other."[5]

CHAPTER 6
YOU MIGHT HAVE A BALANCE
PROBLEM

EVERY TOMORROW HAS TWO HANDLES. WE
CAN TAKE HOLD OF IT WITH THE HANDLE OF
ANXIETY OR THE HANDLE OF FAITH.

—HENRY WARD BEECHER

The World Christian Encyclopedia says there are more than
30,000 Christian denominations in 238 countries, most of
them developing in the last 500 years. Some consist of only
one or two congregations; others include tens of thousands
of churches. Somehow, they have each made a meaningful distinction between themselves and the other 29,999
denominations. Each group has a distinct way of thinking
about the faith, a set of values it deems non-negotiable.
Each has a distinct expectation of what the group's sanctuary should look like and what its music should sound like.
And each has a set of tools it uses to maintain and sustain
its faith. Group members define themselves by what they
think, what they value, what they do, and how they do it.

The call of the church has always been to organize in a
way that makes sense within a particular cultural context.
Denominations didn't always exist. They were the best
answer for a particular question. Education wings weren't
a given. They were a response to a changing set of values.

THE CHALLENGE FOR CHURCHES IN THE INVENTIVE AGE IS TO RESPOND TO THE RISE OF A CREATIVE, PARTICIPATORY, INCLUSIVE CULTURE.

The challenge for churches in the Inventive Age is to respond to the rise of a creative, participatory, inclusive culture. We must do so in ways that allow us to collaborate with the rest of society. We can only do that when we recognize the limitations of our current cultural patterns.

Every church holds the four cultural components in tension. Ideally, there is balance between the four. But as you'll see, that's rarely the case.

THE GREAT DIVIDE ISN'T SO GREAT AFTER ALL

The four components fall into two broader categories:

IDEAS (THE HEAD AND HEART)

OBJECTS (THE GUT AND HANDS)

American Christianity in the 21st century also seems to be split into two general camps:

EVANGELICAL/PENTECOSTAL (E/P)

DENOMINATIONAL/MAINLINE (D/M)

It doesn't take much effort to see that the Evangelical/ Pentecostal faction works to preserve the ideas half of the quadrant, while the Denominational/Mainline group preserves the objects half.

Neither group has it all right. But neither group has it completely wrong, either. In fact, the only way any of us will survive in the Inventive Age is if we are willing to be people of collaboration and participation and consider that other groups have something to teach us.

We tend to think that the E/P crowd and the D/M crowd are so opposed to one another that they can never find common ground. One is conservative; one is liberal. One is stuck in old ideas; the other is too quick to capitulate to culture. One is right; one is left. Ours is right; theirs is wrong.

The truth is, both groups hold tightly to one half of the grid and have no problem leaving the other open to innovation, change, and reinvention. Our differences are not so much about Christianity as they are about culture.

The Evangelical/Pentecostal folks are often highly creative in the look and feel of their buildings. They adopt various musical styles for worship. They are comfortable with casually dressed pastors and parishioners. They are often the first to utilize new technology—think about the way evangelicals have capitalized on radio, books, television, and the Internet. They are open in how and when they meet— church services might be held on Saturday nights, Sunday afternoons, Tuesdays at 6. They will meet in bars, theaters, warehouses, and homes. The aesthetics and the tools are always open for discussion.

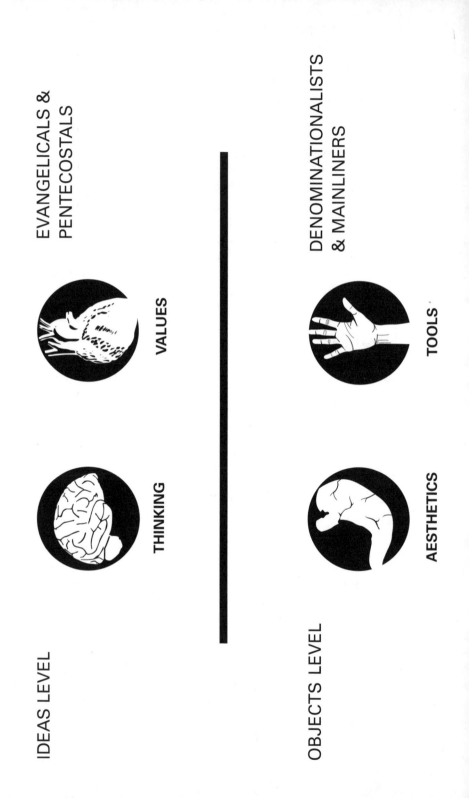

But when it comes to knowledge and values, the innovation tends to stop. I talk to people who tell me, "We can change the package but not the product," or, "The methods should change but the message must always stay the same." Changes on the Ideas side of the grid are seen as a threat to the gospel itself.

Denominational/Mainline folks tend to hold their understanding and values with an open hand. They are the ones voting on homosexual clergy and debating gay marriage. They were the first to ordain women and to blend denominations rather than break off into smaller factions. They don't have statements of faith or codes of conduct. They work hard to use inclusive language for God and each other. They have planted churches all over the world that are culturally sensitive in their portrayal of the gospel.

But when it comes to the objects side of the church, it can be as rigid and fundamentalist as any other. The layout of the church building is sacrosanct—the pulpit goes here, the lectern there. Words and songs and colors carry deep meaning and they are not to be tampered with.

Both the E/P side and the D/M side find themselves with the same problem in the Inventive Age: they tell one story but live another. And because of that, their message of hope and redemption for all people suffers.

When they speak of inclusion but limit participation to the ordained, the message suffers. When they speak of a living, vibrant faith but do so in a building in which the lighting must meet the approval of the elder board, the message suffers. When they speak of the priesthood of all believers but prevent half of those believers from teaching because of their gender, the message suffers.

This is due, in large part, to the ages in which these groups came of age. The E/P side was well suited for the age in which it was born—the Information Age. These churches tend to emphasize doctrine and morality because they reflect an age when the culture valued knowledge and information. It was important to know your theology, to know your statement of faith, to know why you believed what you believed.

In the same way, the D/M side was well suited for the Industrial Age. The emphasis on ritual and repeatability, the focus on creating a particular look that communicated a denominational standard, grew out of a culture that rewarded new tools and new ways of building a better product.

The challenges facing the church in the Inventive Age provide a common starting ground for the Evangelical/Pentecostal side and the Denominational/Mainline side. We are all living with systems that are out of balance, that tilt heavily toward one side of the quadrant while pretending the other side doesn't matter.

Finding a balance between the four cultural components will do more than help churches function in the Inventive Age. It will heal the rifts that exist among God's people.

ADJUSTING YOUR COMPONENTS FOR SOUND

Getting the balance of head, heart, gut, and hands just right takes some fiddling with the knobs. If you let one take over the others, you end up with a distorted message. You have to understand how they play out to get the calibration right.

Head/Knowledge

The Ideas side of the quadrant can be the more difficult side to exegete. So much of it is assumption and unspoken expectation.

I was well into my seminary experience when I first heard the phrase "KJO is the only way to go." I didn't know what "KJO" referred to so I didn't know what to make of that statement. Once I learned that KJO stood for "King James Only," I was certain it was not the only way to go.

The way we think about the world matters. The story we tell about the world matters. The words we use to tell that story matter. In the church we often use a strange language for ordinary things—vestry, sanctuary, pulpit. In other places these are called a storage room, a meeting space, and a place to put your notes. But we believe these things have special meaning in the church so we use special words for them.

That's what language does. It communicates intention and creates a way of thinking.

The King James Only people want certain verses to be worded in a particular way. This became clear to me in a conversation about God's involvement in our lives.

Some KJO friends and I were talking about Romans 8:28. The King James version reads, "And we know that *all things work together for good* to them that love God. . . ." They took this passage to mean that God is responsible for all things. The Bible translation I had says, "And we know that *in all things God works* for the good of those who love him. . . ." I take it to mean that God is engaged in all things.

In the translation I used, the thing didn't need to be good; God would make it good. In the King James Version, the things work for good. That's why my KJO friends look for causality in the face of crisis. I ask, "What good thing will God bring out of this tragedy?" They ask, "Why did God make this happen?" They believe there must be some good intention behind a seemingly evil occurrence.

The words lead to a worldview. And that matters.

Belief is funny. It is so important and yet we have so little control over it. None of us chooses our native language. We learn it from the people around us. We don't choose our hermeneutics; we inherit them from those who teach us the faith.

In 1988 I played basketball in an international tournament in Nicaragua. One of the other teams was from the Soviet Union. We Americans had been raised to consider Soviets the enemy. (I was still enraptured with visions of *Rocky IV* where Rocky takes on Ivan Drago, the Soviet "killing machine.") All we really knew about them is that they were the people with the bombs aimed at us.

One evening I ended up talking to a Russian player named Anatoly. I didn't know any Russian and Anatoly knew only a bit of English, so we spoke through a translator. I remember being struck by the realization that it was only circumstance that made Anatoly and me different. Had I been born in the Soviet Union, I would be just like Anatoly. I would speak Russian. I would be a practicing atheist. I would wonder about the possibility of political freedom. I would have grown up thinking of Americans as the enemy.

Worldviews matter. But they can change. My parents grew up with the A-bomb. I grew up with the nuclear bomb. My kids are growing up with suicide bombs. Our enemies have changed. Our fears have changed. It seems to me our hopes and dreams and expectations can change, too.

 ### Heart/Values

I recently led a conference for Christian Reformed pastors on the practice of community participation in sermons—something we've been doing at Solomon's Porch since the beginning. I suggested they make time in their services for their congregants to ask questions about the sermon, to offer their input, and to share their thoughts on what they had heard. One man, who was the head of the worship committee at his church, raised his hand and said, "First Corinthians 14 admonishes us to have orderly meetings. How is that possible with this model?"

BELIEF IS FUNNY. IT IS SO IMPORTANT AND YET WE HAVE SO LITTLE CONTROL OVER IT.

His understanding of "orderly" is that one well-prepared person should speak for a determined amount of time. I explained that in our community, the value is having as many voices as possible contribute to the conversation. We organize our gatherings around that value. For us, that is "fitting and orderly."

Both of us want to be faithful to Paul's admonition. Where we differ is in our values.

So much of what consumes churches in Evangelical/Pentecostal circles falls under the umbrella of values. Think about the committee meetings you've sat in. I'm willing to bet most of them center not on doctrine, but on values.

There are those who hold that the only true form of prayer is extemporaneous free-form prayer. A written prayer strikes them as false, phony even.

There are those who hold that prayer is so important, so sacred, that it needs to be thought-out and well prepared.

They believe the prayers written centuries ago speak to the rich tradition of our faith. A prayer off the top of your head can never match the theological depth of those historic words.

So which is it? Is prayer so important that it should come from the heart? Or is it so important it should be written down?

In some churches, financial issues are considered part of the life of the community and they are talked about during the worship services. In others, money is something to be dealt with privately. What seem to be conflicts about money are really conflicts about the value of privacy.

I worked at a church where we built a $10 million worship center. While the building itself was the subject of much conversation, the big point of contention was the organ. A small group of people in the church wanted us to have a first-class contemporary organ. They contributed the $1 million needed to build a magnificent organ. They believed God should have our very best.

There were, however, a number of young people in the church who were bothered by what they saw as a waste of money. They believed the money would be better spent caring for the poor. They couldn't understand why an organ should be a higher priority than food and shelter for the "least of these."

This was not an issue of one group being more faithful than the other. It was an issue of what they valued. Both groups wanted to be part of God's work in the world. Where they differed was on how to do that.

Our biggest challenges come when we assume that those who hold worldviews or values that differ from ours *lack* knowledge or values.

Gut/Aesthetics

I never knew a couch could create such a stir.

At Solomon's Porch, our gathering space is filled with couches. There are a few armchairs around, some end tables, a couple of coffee tables and lamps, but most of the space is occupied by couches.

If people know nothing else about our community, they seem to know about the couches. I know people in our church who, when trying to describe our community to others, start with "We sit on couches." I get more questions about those couches than just about anything else.

Having spent most of my Christian life in the Evangelical/ Pentecostal conversation, I knew how important ideas were. I had no idea objects were such a big deal.

But they are. The aesthetics of our churches communicate as much about who we are and what we believe as any sermon or doctrine or theology.

We use couches because we want people to feel at home. Other churches use theater-style seating because they think people are most comfortable when they have their own spaces, when it's clear who is sitting where. Other churches use pews because they want to create a focal point for the service—the pulpit, the altar, or both.

Every element of our spaces, our music, the time we meet, the mood we create, the people we include, points to our values.

If you want to know how important aesthetics are in your community, rearrange the furniture, paint a wall, change the music, wear jeans—or stop wearing jeans—and see what happens.

Adam was a worship leader at a fast growing contempo-
rary church where the message was "come as you are."
Come as you are was printed on the top of the bulletin just
under the name of the church. It was one of the first phrases used in the welcome portion of the Sunday service. It
was on the bulk mailing that went to every household in a
three-mile radius of the church.

Adam believed this message applied to him as well. He
was young and the church liked the vitality and passion
he brought to his job. He played guitar like a pro and the
senior pastor tapped his foot along to Adam's music. He
introduced his songs with stories from his life and people
nodded approvingly. He was himself and it was great.

AESTHETICS ARE POWERFUL.

One Sunday, the sermon was based on the Scripture passage describing Moses interacting with God at Mount
Sinai. Before he sang, Adam reread the words from Exo-
dus: "Take off your sandals, for the place where you are
standing is holy ground." Adam proceeded to take of his
shoes and socks as he led into the next worship song. He
thought it was a meaningful gesture. He was wrong.

After the service the senior pastor said to him, "If you ever
take your shoes off again while you're leading music, that
will be your last song as our worship leader!" Adam was
stunned. He didn't understand what he'd done wrong. The
pastor explained, "It's just dirty and uncouth to be in front
of people with your toes showing. People will not respect
you and follow you."

Aesthetics are powerful.

We rent our building from the Methodist denomination,
but we have free reign to make it our own. When we

moved in, all the walls were white. Every wall in every room and every hallway—white.

We had moved from a warehouse where we'd painted every surface we could find, so we wanted to add some color to our new space. We opened up the painting process to the community, asking people to choose a room or a hall or a closet and paint it. There was no master plan to the color scheme of the building. People who had adjoining spaces might consult each other, but it was essentially a free-for-all.

Within a week of moving in, we had nearly every room—including the three-story sanctuary—painted.

A month or so later a few members of the Methodist congregation that had met in the church for decades stopped in to say hello. One of the women, Kay, immediately noticed all the color and said, "Oh my, you've added so much color to the place! How long did it take you to make all these decisions?" I told her about our uncoordinated collective effort. Kay just shook her head and said, "I was on the building committee for 8 years and in all that time the only color we could agree on was white."

I've had my own jarring aesthetic moments. Not long ago, I visited a church with a good friend of mine. I felt perfectly at home until we started singing. That's when the happy clappy stuff started. I just don't get that. I don't understand raising your hands up in the air when you sing. I don't understand people jumping up and down and dancing in the aisles. It's as foreign to me as our crazy wall colors were to Kay.

The color of the walls really matters to some people. The seating really matters. The lighting and the music and the dancing and the stained glass really matter. Aesthetics are highly personal and highly reflective of our values and beliefs. We have to recognize that not everyone shares our sensibilities and that we might, to quote the great Ricky Ricardo, have some 'splainin' to do when new people show up. At the same time, we need to be careful about dismissing the aesthetics of others as frivolous or meaningless. To do so is to dismiss the power of aesthetics to enrich and enliven our faith.

Hands/Tools

Several years ago, a friend told me about a growing tension at his Presbyterian church. The church had made the decision to add a projection screen to its sanctuary. Congregants wanted to use new kinds of music, the kind that wasn't in their hymnals.

What began as a simple decision to use a new tool soon became a far more contentious issue.

Initially there was backlash over the placement of the screen. It needed to be somewhere everyone could see it, but it couldn't distract from the iconic symbols in the church. Should they cover the stained glass window above the choir or the cross just below the window? Aesthetically, this new tool and the neoclassic architecture of the building were fairly incompatible.

Tools seem like they should be the most innocuous part of the quadrant. Clearly, that's not the case. Often, they are the most powerful.

The Protestant Reformation never would have taken place without the invention of the printing press. That tool eventually allowed ordinary people to get copies of the Bible in their native languages. It was a key component to the social changes in the church.

The rise in literacy during the early 20th century created

a "printing press" kind of change in the church as well, moving it from the Industrial Age into the Information Age. Pastors, who were once the most educated people in the church, were now leading, teaching, and inspiring a highly educated congregation. People didn't have to come to church to hear the Word of God, they could read it for themselves any time and any place they wanted to. The tool of the book changed the role of the pastor and the role of the church.

"We are still a book church," Gwen confessed at a pastors' round-table lunch. "We read and sing from a book and not the wall." All the other pastors confessed that they used projectors for the lyrics of their songs and were, therefore, wall people or, as one put it, "off-the-wall" singers. Gwen noted that her church would never go to the wall model because of their aesthetic values. "Many of our people like to see the music notes as they sing. It helps us sing more complicated music." Gwen's community recognized that if you move from the book to the wall, you make changes that go far beyond where people look when they sing.

Tools change everything.

The tool of the moment is the Internet. Nothing says "We're an Inventive Age church!" like a robust website, a podcast, and a Facebook fan page. But the tool of the Internet creates as much chaos for churches as putting up a screen in a neoclassical sanctuary. Changing the tool changes so much more.

I recently received an e-mail announcement that read, "Central Christian Church in Las Vegas recently became the world's first church to launch a Facebook campus. The online campus features six live services per week, complete with live lobby chat, tithing, and teaching. The church hopes to capture some of the 250 million Facebook users. The inaugural service had 450 attendees from around the globe. Central Christian now has four physical campuses and two virtual campuses—one on their website and one on Facebook."

The people at Central Christian Church see the tool of the Internet as a way of connecting with (or, in the words of the press release, "capture") people who spend time online. And that might be true. But what the folks at Central are sure to find is that this new tool will impact their entire system.

It will create the need for new content and that might lead to new staff positions which will lead to new financial issues which will lead to changes in their discussions about money which will lead to conversations about what they value and on and on and on.

It will lead to new interactions: having a "global" church means having global sensitivities and an understanding of how people in other places think and understand the world and the gospel.

It will involve new aesthetic sensibilities: When your congregation is on a Facebook page, do you use music? Do you design your page or use the Facebook template? If you create a design, which culture's aesthetic should you incorporate?

As Inventive Age as a Facebook church seems on the surface, it won't last long if it doesn't allow for participation, for collaboration and beauty and creativity.

Modern denominations are a particular organization tool created in the midst of Industrial Age. They were created not only to systematize and standardize a collection of churches, but to create a support system for pastors as well. Before the advent of health insurance and pension systems, being a pastor was a risky job with little, if any, pay.

Denominations helped professionalize ministry jobs. They made it possible for churches in the Information Age to bring on Teaching Pastors and Youth Pastors and Children's Pastors and Worship Pastors. They offered insurance and retirement plans and professional growth opportunities. They made being a pastor a secure job. Those tools—the denomination, the insurance, the retirement plans—still hold sway over pastors. I have had denominational pastors tell me that the only reason they stay with the organization is because of the benefits.

Tools change everything.

CREATING HARMONY

The Inventive Age, defined by the emphasis on cooperation, participation, beauty, organic growth, and user-friendliness, demands we re-evaluate our understanding, our values, our aesthetics, and our tools. If our churches are going to remain relevant in a culture that is shifting rapidly, we have to be willing to shift along with it.

TOOLS CHANGE EVERYTHING.

That doesn't mean every church has to be wired up. It doesn't mean you have to scrap the hymnals and dump the pews. It means you need to know what you're holding on to and why. You need to know who you are and what makes you that way. You need to have your head, heart, gut, and hands working together, not pulling against one another.

I was at a conference recently where a number of pastors were quite vocal about the need to use gender-neutral language for God. They wanted to make sure their words were inclusive. But I was taken aback by how many of these folks still practiced institutionalized forms of exclusion. For some it was through a system of ordination that limits who can perform particular activities in church. Others were involved in more subtle structures that determine who can be in leadership, who can serve communion, who can preach a sermon. They were negating their own desires.

My friend Rachel, who is part of what she calls the "scratch and sniff" tradition of Christianity (the kind that uses incense, gestures, such as crossing oneself, and particular hymns at particular times of the year), said to me recently, "You know at my church we allow queers like me to be full participants in the community. But if someone uses the wrong colored tablecloth for the season you would think the world was about to end." The balance is off. The way to get the balance back isn't to start limiting participation or suggest that the colors don't matter. It's to rethink it all and find ways to be people who value both.

The faith communities that thrive in the Inventive Age will be those that figure out how to create and keep a harmonious balance between the four components.

As you look at your community, ask yourselves a few questions:

WHAT ARE THE PLACES OF COHESION?

WHAT ARE THE PLACES OF CONFLICT?

ARE OUR VALUES OUT OF SYNCH WITH OUR BELIEFS?

ARE OUR AESTHETICS COMMUNICATING ONE THING WHILE OUR DOCTRINE IS COMMUNICATING ANOTHER?

ARE OUR TOOLS HELPING US BE THE COMMUNITY WE WANT TO BE?

Once you know where you sit on the quadrant, you have to be willing to adjust not only those things you are comfortable changing but those that scare you. And we have to be willing to cross-pollinate, to give generously from what we know, and to accept the gifts of change others bring to us.

As I was putting this book together, I met with some people from Solomon's Porch to talk through the ideas and get their feedback. As we worked through the four components, we tried to place some of the things that make us "us" in their places. Naturally, we started with the couches.

At first, it seemed obvious that they were an expression of our aesthetic. But then we talked about how they are really part of our value system—we value people feeling like they are among friends and family, feeling at home in our space. This value comes out of our understanding of Christian community, our belief that a church is not just a group of people who meet once a week to listen to a lecture but a group of people who are intentional about sharing life together. We considered that maybe the couches are a tool we use to communicate that message to people, something we use to accomplish our goals.

It turns out our couches, most of which are other people's castoffs, are beautiful examples of our effort to balance the head, heart, gut, and hands of our community. We don't have it all figured out, but those couches? For us, they are just about perfect.

CHAPTER 7
ARE YOU A HYBRID CAR?

> WE DON'T SEE THINGS AS THEY ARE; WE
> SEE THEM AS WE ARE.
>
> —ANAIS NIN

Creating harmony between the head, heart, guts, and hands of your community starts with knowing who you are. But that's not where it stops. The Inventive Age—like every age before it—demands we adjust our thinking, or understanding, our values, our aesthetics, and our tools so that we can live out the call to be the people of God in this place and time.

It is no longer sufficient to be a gathering space for a flock of neighbors. It is no longer enough to put a denominational brand on a group of people. It is no longer desirable to make sure people walk out the door with proper knowledge. The church has to be about remaking culture. We have to be about knowing the questions of the Inventive Age and figuring out how to make sense of them.

In every age, the culture rewards and reinforces particular characteristics—in people and in institutions. In the Agrarian Age, people were rewarded for hard work, for resilience, for persistence. In the Industrial Age it was the ability to fit into a system and contribute to the whole that

gave a person a sense of worth. The Information Age rewarded those who could analyze, systematize, and teach.
The Inventive Age will reward those who make, connect,
create, and facilitate.

The qualities that make someone successful in one age
can quickly become liabilities in the next. Hard work made
a difference in farming. In the factory it was efficiency that
mattered, not effort.

THE CHURCH HAS TO BE ABOUT REMAKING CULTURE.

That doesn't mean the ages past have nothing for us. In
fact, there is much to be admired, even adopted, from
those epochs. The emphasis on creativity that marks the
Inventive Age has brought with it a renewed interest in
true craftsmanship that shows up in everything from
houses to furniture to music to food. There is a shift away
from large churches that bring in people from a large met-
ropolitan area and toward a kind of parish model in which
a church sees itself as investing in a particular neighborhood. There is a continued interest in learning, in educat-
ing, in discovery and mastery.

Yet each of these values bears the hallmarks of the Inventive Age. Our handcrafted houses are built with the latest
in green materials and technologies. Our local churches
are meeting in coffee shops and refurbished Industrial Age
church buildings. Our education is happening online at the
user's own pace and schedule.

I know there are churches that function just fine living as

Agrarian Age churches or Industrial Age churches or Information Age churches. But you're reading this book because things aren't just fine.

There is tension in your community, something you can't quite put your finger on. Your congregation is dying out or disengaged. You see a generation of people who are leaving churches like yours and heading to who knows where. You know something needs to change but you don't want—or aren't able—to be a coffee shop church or a church with couches or a church of 20-somethings.

Imagine where we'd be if farmers stopped farming at the end of the Agrarian Age. Thankfully, they didn't stop. They adapted. They figured out how to utilize the best of the Industrial Age—like expanded transportation and distribution options—to make farming a sustainable and necessary part of the culture. When the Information Age came along, they were able to expand their farms, discover new crops, exchange information, and refine their practices by applying the best characteristics of the age to their work. In the Inventive Age, farmers are finding themselves facing challenges Agrarian Age farmers never imagined. But I believe they will continue to adapt, to harness the creative impulses of this age for their benefit.

The church needs to follow suit. We need to adapt to our culture or risk falling by the wayside.

THE INVENTIVE AGE WILL REWARD THOSE WHO MAKE, CONNECT, AND FACILITATE.

The way I see it, churches have three options for moving forward: we can exist *for* the Inventive Age, *with* the Inventive Age, or *as* the Inventive Age.

The hybrid car is not an entirely new invention. It's old technology mixed with new. The electric car, on the other hand, that's new. Both work. Both get you from point A to point B. But you have to know the difference. You need to know which one you're driving.

Churches that choose to exist *for* the Inventive Age and *with* the Inventive Age need to be who they are and figure out how the Inventive Age will impact them. Churches that choose to function *as* Inventive Age churches need to know how they connect to previous ages and must be willing to carry the best of those ages with them as they move forward.

YOUR MISSIONARY POSITION

There are places in Africa, China, and South America where people who have very little in common with you and me gather at 11:00 on a Sunday morning and sit in rows of benches that face one direction. They listen to a sermon from a man standing at a pulpit. They sing songs that were written 200 years ago in Europe and played on electric organs. They do this because they were taught that this is what church looks like. It doesn't look like anything else they have seen or feel like anything else they have done, but it's church. This is what ministry *for* a culture looks like. It takes what we know and sets it down in the middle of a culture. You could say it's like driving an SUV when gas costs four bucks a gallon.

There are other places in the world where missionaries come to a village or a city and engage the local people in ministry. They spend time at other communal gatherings and figure out what kind of music and seating and gathering spaces are familiar to the people who live there. They use all of this information to create churches that feel at home in the culture but still bear the marks of the organization. This is ministry *with* a culture. It melds a little of this and a little of that to create something that looks a little like both. It's the hybrid car of missions.

There are Christian ministries that go into communities and identify leaders. They equip these leaders to start churches that fit in with their context. The leaders are indigenous, the music—if there is any—is indigenous, the experience is completely driven by the needs and expectations of the culture. This is ministry *as* a culture. It's the electric car—something completely new that simply doesn't run like the previous models.

WE NEED TO ADAPT TO OUR CULTURE OR RISK FALLING BY THE WAYSIDE.

As churches consider how best to live in the Inventive Age, I want to be clear that there isn't one right answer. Because this age carries with it remnants of the previous ages, we need churches that understand where they've come from and know exactly where they fit in the scope of history. We need churches *for* the Inventive Age. We need churches that work *with* the Inventive Age. And we need churches that exist *as* the Inventive Age.

No matter which kind of church you are, you will need to add new understandings, new values, new aesthetic sensibilities, and new tools to those you already have. It won't be easy or comfortable—change never is—but our mission is to be the church in this place and time. We don't have a choice.

CHAPTER 8
BEING THE CHURCH *FOR*
THE INVENTIVE AGE

LOOK BEFORE, OR YOU MIGHT FIND
YOURSELF BEHIND.

—BENJAMIN FRANKLIN

There are churches that work well right now, that are
healthy and vibrant and sustainable. We need those
churches in the Inventive Age.

People in the Inventive Age need history. We are all about the
future, but we are not ignorant of the past. We know there
is a rich tradition of thought and practice behind us and we
long to know about it and carry it with us. We don't want to
limit our connections to people like us. We want to hear the
stories of people from other places, other eras, other mind-
sets. We need to be invited into those conversations.

A church for the Inventive Age is one that welcomes new
people and new ideas, one that knows how to plug people
in and show them how they can contribute.

A friend of mine is doing some consulting for a church
called St. Mark's. St. Mark's is very much an Agrarian Age
church. The church is outfitted with a large, beautiful organ.

The clergy wears stoles and long white robes. The building itself, which was built in the 1930s, bears the architecture of an 18th-century European cathedral. The door is red and any discussion to make it otherwise is a non-starter. They use incense and bells. Liturgical colors mark the passing of the year. The polity of the church is functionally hierarchical — there are ordained clergy members who are set apart for particular tasks. Even though the church is filled with many professional people — medical doctors, lawyers, teachers, professors, accountants — certain roles in the church are still reserved for the clergy as though they are the only people capable of such matters.

My friend believes, and I think she's right, that St. Mark's would lose all its charm and meaning for the people who love it if they were to take on the style and practices of the Inventive Age. She says, "They are really good at this version of the faith and it would be a shame to lose that."

I don't think they have to.

Being a "for" church means saying, "We are here. We welcome you in and hope you benefit from what we have to offer." The Inventive Age needs churches like St. Mark's.

Here's how the head, heart, gut, and hands of a church like St. Mark's can expand to embrace the Inventive Age:

HEAD

Learn the language: Because this is a cross-cultural relationship, one of the most important elements of connection is finding a common language. People of the Inventive Age can either learn the native tongue, or they can teach you their language. But as with all language learning, there will be gaps. There are entire categories of Christian conversation that hold little meaning for people of the Inventive Age. We are less interested in outcomes than processes. If you talk about church growth, we won't get it because that's not the most important sign of church health for us. Remember, language creates understanding and vice versa. If a person from the Inventive Age doesn't know specific ecclesiological terms (like ecclesiology for instance), or doesn't know the significance of particular terms and phrases, she will feel like an outsider. You don't have to change your language, but be ready to translate the words you use and incorporate the language of the Inventive Age.

Lend expertise: Just because we've moved out of the Information Age doesn't mean people no longer value information—there's not a blogger alive who wouldn't love to sit down with Bill Gates. People in the Inventive Age want to know what you know. The knowledge you have, the ways you have sustained your faith over the years, the discoveries you've made along the way—these are invaluable to us. We want our faith to be connected to the trajectory of church history and we can't do that without you. When you see us heading toward murky waters, don't just warn us off or ignore us, tell us what you know. We really will listen.

Of course, you'll have to listen, too. It can be tempting to dismiss the ideas and excitement of Inventive Age people as being change for change's sake. But even when you think we are being ridiculous, listen. Reflect what you hear. Ask questions and encourage deeper thinking. But most of all, listen.

Practice hope: It's a natural human instinct to distrust and dismiss people who are different from us. This is especially true when those people have a different understanding of the world, a different set of values, different aesthetic sensibilities, and different tools. But as we've seen, the head, heart, gut, and hands of your community aren't givens. They aren't universal. Somewhere along the line, someone decided people should be able to read the Bible. That probably sounded like a terrible idea to the powers that be of the day. Aren't you glad someone decided to trust the ordinary people with the Word of God?

EVEN WHEN YOU THINK INVENTIVE AGE PEOPLE ARE BEING RIDICULOUS, LISTEN.

Your confidence and belief in the validity of another person's faith, even if it looks and feels different from yours, can be a tremendous gift. There is so much uncertainty in the Inventive Age. And while that's exciting in all kinds of ways, it can freak some of us out. We need to know that other people see what's good in us, that people who have held on to their faith in times of crisis or doubt hold out hope that we can do the same.

HEART

Be welcoming: Because people in the Inventive Age value participation and collaboration, we want to be part of what you're doing. We have ideas and energy and passion that can be the kind of fresh air nearly every church needs from time to time. We won't understand everything you do and will appreciate you showing us what you're about and inviting us to be part of it. And we will appreciate your curiosity about our experiences as well.

Be authentic and open: People in the Inventive Age want

connection and that can't happen unless people are who they are. Younger people want to see older people being themselves. If someone is drawn to your church, it's because of your music and your setting and your smells and candles. You can add all the couches you want but if your existing congregation isn't comfortable sitting on them, you'll just feel ridiculous. Embrace who you are. Tell your story with honesty and openness. Talk about your challenges. Be vulnerable. Be clear. And when you don't know why your Inventive Age people are doing what they're doing, ask.

Prepare to struggle: The church in the Inventive Age will produce different outcomes than churches of previous ages. People think differently. They hold different values. They have different aesthetic preferences. They use different tools. So the outcomes will be different, too. That can create real struggle in "for" churches.

I was talking with a woman whose church had disbanded. An Inventive Age church was now using the building and she decided to give it a try. She just wasn't sure there was a place for her there. She understood the changes this new church had made and she knew that the people attending the new church wouldn't have fit into the previous community. She saw the good that was happening. But she wanted to know if the people in this new church "still, each individually, went to the Bible to find answers." From what I knew about the church, I believed it was their hope that they would connect to the Bible personally and communally. But I also knew this wasn't the outcome this dear woman hoped for.

She hoped they were having daily, personal encounters with the Bible. I was fairly sure that wasn't the norm. Even though I told her that I was certain this community saw the Bible as important to their faith and authoritative on the issues on which it spoke, she found it hard to give credence to any approach other than what she was used to.

She assured me, and I believed her, that she would try to see that as valid, but it would be hard for her.

These struggles won't go away, but they are worth talking about. Like all assumptions, those that concern faith are less damaging when they are spoken out loud and worked out in the context of trusting relationships.

GUT

Know your strengths: One of the strongest pulls of a church like St. Mark's is the rich sense of tradition and history. For all our focus on the future, people of the Inventive Age love to discover the past. My friend Nadia Boltz-Weber, a Lutheran pastor, talks about how many of the younger people who come to her church are there, at least in part, because of the liturgy. They love the sense of ritual and rhythm it gives to their religious experience. If you're part of a church that sings the words of institution and wafts incense around the room, you don't have to stop in an effort to make room for the Inventive Age. If your aesthetics are authentic expressions of your community, they will be meaningful to people of the Inventive Age.

HANDS

Tell stories: My friends Don and Pam pastor a church in New York. Their church is very much in keeping with the Wesleyan tradition. Don and Pam were part of a Methodist church and knew the story of the Wesley brothers, John and Charles, who responded to the great changes in the Anglican church of the late 18th century. The brothers were in the United States, watching how the changing face of this new nation was challenging the church. When they returned to England, the brothers started preaching stations and missions outposts outside of the established church. These efforts led to the birth of the Methodist Church in England and, eventually, in the United States.

This story inspired Don and Pam to follow in the footsteps of John Wesley and create a new expression of Christianity that fit their time and place.

It's easy for people of the Inventive Age to think they have discovered fire when they have simply found something new to light. Your stories remind us of what's come before and inspire us to follow that path of creativity and faithfulness.

CHAPTER 9
BEING THE CHURCH *WITH*
THE INVENTIVE AGE

I WANT TO KNOW WHAT BECAME OF THE
CHANGES WE WAITED FOR LOVE TO BRING.
WERE THEY ONLY THE FITFUL DREAMS OF
SOME GREATER AWAKENING?

—JACKSON BROWNE, "THE PRETENDER"

The leadership of First Presbyterian invited me to join
them for breakfast. They were interested in starting a
"church-within-a-church" ministry to appeal to young
adults, and they wanted my thoughts on how they should
proceed. This is a classic "with" model. The church itself
was just fine. But they saw a demographic that seemed to
want and need a different kind of church experience. They
didn't have a name for it, but what they had noticed was
the shift from the Information Age to the Inventive Age.

The assumption was that if they had a worship service
with a younger vibe and staff people who were part of the
desired demographic, a new generation of people would
find a home at the church. They knew the church as a
whole was not ready for the kinds of changes this new effort would bring, but they wanted to "live together" to see
what kind of effect they could have on one another. Their
hope was that by living with each other, both the young

adults and the older congregation would benefit. It was a worthy goal.

My advice to them didn't involve the details of this new ministry. I spent most of my time talking about the "mother" church and what they needed to do to make this relationship work. I explained that they were entering into a process that would at times require them to live in ways that might be a bit counterintuitive. This wasn't like their ministry efforts for children or even teenagers where they had created something that ran by its own rules while still falling completely under the auspices of the church. This relationship required a completely different set of expectations and skills.

Their experiment lasted five years and then, unfortunately, ended with much tension. For the most part, my suggestions became impossible for them to follow. Like any parent-child (or adult-child) relationship, the tension between freedom and responsibility became too much for either party to bear.

That's why the "with" option is, I find, the most difficult way forward. But if the church sets up clear expectations—and sticks to them—before making a move, it can work.

Here's how the head, heart, gut, and hands of a church can expand to partner with people of the Inventive Age:

HEAD

Walk alongside: Walking alongside someone is different than walking in front of her and leading the way, or walking behind her and pushing. It means going at the same pace and sharing the experience. It can be incredibly difficult, particularly for churches that have been successful in some way. There's an urge to offer advice, to guide, to share expertise. But those are disastrous in a "with" relationship. I've seen too many "with" efforts fail because the main church kept offering suggestions or ideas or usurping leadership. I've seen them fail because the leadership of the founding church saw something working in the new ministry, used it in the main church setting, watched it fail, then explained to the new ministry that this idea was faulty and should be dropped. I've seen it fail because of unspoken expectations that led churches to push new ministries into places they weren't ready to go. The only way the "with" arrangement works is if there is less leadership and more companionship.

Become the learner: If your church truly believes there is a need to minister to people of the Inventive Age, then you have to accept that they have something to offer you in return. "With" churches need to have an even broader posture of openness and welcome than "for" churches because you are trying to become equal partners. Think about the missionaries who spend time talking to the native people before they start up a ministry. They don't roll in and create something they think the people need. They listen. They learn. And only then do they begin.

Know who's who: Walking alongside another leader is a strange position for those of us who are used to being in charge. It's like parenting an adult child. When do you pick up the check? When do you step in? When do you let them fail? When do you allow them to offer input on what you're doing? If you have charged someone with the leadership of a new ministry, then you have to let her lead. Find out what she needs from you and what you need from her, then abide by that conversation.

Trust: The "with" approach requires a great deal of trust from both groups. Your church needs to trust that the new ministry won't take advantage of you. You need to trust that they will find their footing. You need to trust the leadership and stay out of their way. And they need to trust you. They need to trust your commitment to this endeavor. They need to trust that you will let them make mistakes without pulling the plug on the whole thing.

In the case of the Presbyterian church, it was their mutual trust that allowed them five years of ministry and preserved the friendship among the parties involved even when the relationship between their communities ended.

HEART

Set aside authenticity: This is one of those counterintuitive parts. But if you think like a parent for a minute, you'll see what I mean. Kids make us mad. They do things that make us want to yell and scold and shut them in their rooms for months. They do things that are so stupid, so unreasonable that we wonder if they've ever listened to a word we've said. But we don't say all of that to them. We keep our mouths shut and stay calm. We figure out that kids don't need to know everything we think, especially when it concerns them and their decision-making abilities. We know we will do more harm than good if we express every disappointment and frustration we feel about the decisions they make.

Look away: A "with" church has to be willing to look the other way when the Inventive Age church wants to try something out of your comfort zone. They might want to invite people who act or dress differently from your other congregants. They might want to drink wine or beer at a church function. They might want to let people who have never been to seminary preach a sermon or lead a class. They might have ideas about the role of women or the importance of sexuality or the solemnity of communion that mess with every value you hold. If something concerns you, ask about it, learn more, assume good intentions. Their approach might be a train wreck. But they'll figure that out. You have to know when to look away.

Be prepared for allergic reactions: I've started using this language of allergies to talk about the way people often feel about change. Like most allergies, change is rarely life-threatening, but it can be very uncomfortable. It can make us itchy and irritable. There will be parts of the "with" relationship that irritate you, that make you tired, that make you wish it would just go away. So, like an asthmatic in the spring, prepare yourself.

A woman I know was facilitating a "with" effort in her church. The start-up church had its own staff, but she was always invited to join their meetings. She went for a while, but she told me she'd stopped going because the meetings were run in a way that made all of her cultural value allergies kick in. "They wasted so much time! They always started late. There was a lack of concern for properly documenting the decisions. . . ." She could see the value of this people-centered, laid-back approach. But it worried her and led her to ask questions that began to get in the way of the relationship. In light of her allergic reaction, she adjusted her involvement.

GUT

Divorce your furniture: Maybe it's because "with" churches tend to be "objects" churches, or maybe it's because aesthetics reflect values, but I find that aesthetics are often the biggest challenge in the "with" relationship. To make this partnership work, you have to end your commitment to a particular style of music, a particular set up of the room, a particular dress code or smell or kind of art. You might have fantastic reasons for wanting the chairs to stay where they are or for people to park on a certain side of the street. You might have well-informed opinions on how to fit more people into a space or lead people in meaningful worship. It doesn't matter. Because the understanding and values that led you to your sense of what church should look like and feel like are different than the understanding and values of the Inventive Age people with whom you are trying to connect. They want to know you. They want to build community with you. But they don't want to know why your way is better.

Get in tune with the vibe: When the planning team at The Bible Church outside of Dallas was building a new worship sanctuary they made sure 80 percent of their planning group was made up of people with Inventive Age sensibilities. Certainly they valued the input of the other 20 percent, but they also recognized that if they wanted to build something for the Inventive Age, they needed the pushback of people who had a whole different set of ideas about what church could look and feel like. For 20 percent of the group, the previous iteration of church had been acceptable. For 80 percent, it was acceptable, but not preferable. The leadership of the church knew the only way to keep the power of what is from crushing the power of what could be was to stack the deck.

People in the Inventive Age have ideas—lots and lots of ideas—about what kinds of music and lighting and furniture and architecture create the vibe they are looking for in a church. These ideas help them define themselves and their expressions of faith. Don't get in the way.

HANDS

Lend resources: When it comes to church, the biggest challenge for people of the Inventive Age is not a lack of motivation or ideas. It's the lack of resources. If you've got Inventive Age people at your church, it's not primarily because of your ideas. It's because you have resources that are meaningful to them. So share them. Give generously of your space, your equipment, even your money if necessary. This is difficult posture for a lot of churches. It demands intense humility and a willingness to hold your "stuff" with a loose grip. Show your belief in this group of people by giving them what they need to express their faith in ways that mean something to them. If they need advice, they'll ask for it.

A few years ago, when Solomon's Porch was between buildings, we shared a church with two other congregations. On Sunday nights, we'd pull a few of our couches into the sanctuary—which was filled with pews—just to make it feel like home. The gracious people at the church held their building loosely, giving us space to keep a few lamps and couches and paintings in their overflow area so we could maintain a sense of identity in this new relationship. It was a small concession on their part that made a big impression on us.

Avoid all strings: People of the Inventive Age are experimental. They will try something without having all the pieces in place to make it work. If you're in a "with" relationship with an Inventive Age community, the cycle of a new idea coming to life then falling apart can be exhausting. I've seen churches respond to this cycle by requiring something akin to a business plan from groups hoping to start a "with" expression of faith. When the group veers off the plan or the plan simply doesn't work, the parent church cuts off the relationship and chalks it up to wrongheaded ideology.

The "with" relationship is healthiest when there are no strings, when money, time, resources, prayer, and support are given unconditionally. Oak Baptist Church had a growing number of Inventive Age people getting involved in their community and they knew they needed to find a way to address the needs and desires of this group. When some of these Inventive Age people wanted to start an experimental community, Oak Baptist gave them half of their building. This became The Pathway Project. There was no expectation that the building be used a certain way or that the group report back to the leadership at Oak Baptist. It was a gift given freely. The Pathway Project used the church basement to hold their worship meetings, to house a regular farmers' market, and to host a tutoring program. The project lasted for three years. The people who started it stuck around and are still part of the Oak Baptist community.

Churches that do the "with" relationship well often end up becoming separate congregations for all the right reasons. Churches that struggle to make it work can find the relationship ending with pain and dashed hopes. No matter which direction the "with" relationship goes, the parenting church needs to be committed to the people involved. They aren't a mission field. They aren't a demographic. They are part of your community.

A healthy "with" relationship calls for a particular posture. It's not easy and it's not for those who want things to happen quickly or smoothly. But for churches willing to move gently into a relationship with people of the Inventive Age, a "with" connection can be a meaningful experience for all involved.

CHAPTER 10
BEING THE CHURCH *AS*
THE INVENTIVE AGE

DON'T ASK WHAT THE WORLD NEEDS. ASK
WHAT MAKES YOU COME ALIVE, AND GO
DO IT. BECAUSE WHAT THE WORLD NEEDS IS
PEOPLE WHO HAVE COME ALIVE.

—HOWARD THURMAN

As I put this final section of the book together, I knew I couldn't just sit in my living room and tell the stories I already know. This part of the book had to be open-sourced. So I put out a request for stories on my network—my blog, Twitter, and Facebook. The stories started rolling in. So the people you are about to meet are real. They are doing this work right now. They are the church in the Inventive Age.

Kimberly Knight works for The Beatitude Society, a progressive Christian network for justice, compassion, and peace. She is also the pastor of Koinonia Congregational Church.

Koinonia doesn't meet in a church building or a coffee shop or a warehouse. Koinonia is part of a revolutionary Internet software program called Second Life, which allows users to socialize and use voice and text chat in real time. Each week, the members of Koinonia—who live all over the world—meet for worship in the 3D-rendered sanctuary where their avatars gather for fellowship, prayer, music, and a sermon. The church follows a liturgical calendar, so members celebrate feasts and festivals that have been part of Christianity for centuries. Here's how she describes it:

> Imagine a new town emerging on the outskirts of your city, a planned village filled with all manner of retail, rolling golf courses, nightclubs, and civic arrangements necessary to organizing a small city. You'd also expect to find houses of worship where the new town's citizens can connect with God and with each other. So it is with the new metropolis of the Internet: churches are springing up every day online, and I am one of the ministers. I am the Circuit Rider but my tools are quite different than the well-worn saddle and leather-bound Bibles of my forebears. My tools are the currency of the online world: Twitter, Facebook, LinkedIn and Second Life. How does a seminary graduate end up as an online Circuit Rider? Answer: I genuinely believe in online community and I see it in practice as the pastor of an online church, Koinonia Congregational Church of Second Life.

Remember the Facebook church I mentioned in chapter 5? It might be on to something great. But I'm not sure it has captured the true nature of the Inventive Age the way Koinonia has. Kimberly has not handed leadership over to the entire virtual community. She is leading through facilitation, not domination. This church is not a wide open, anything goes experiment, but one with an almost tribal sense of community. It is a safe place for expression and connection because there is a framework in which to explore and dream and create.

Making predictions about what will and won't be needed

as we rethink church in the Inventive Age is a little like working for the National Weather Service. I can make some broad predictions for the next stretch, but everything could change in six months. Like planning a summer wedding outdoors, being the church in the Inventive Age means taking your chances and constantly being prepared to change course.

Here are the characteristics I believe distinguish the head, heart, gut, and hands of Inventive Age churches:

HEAD

They exist in perpetual beta: The understanding of perpetual beta is well known in the technology and software fields. In these environments, improvements need to happen in real time, with user input—you can't just shut down a search engine while you refine it. Sometimes a program stays in the beta development stage for an extended or even indefinite period of time. The program is always moving, always developing, always responding to the needs of the users. It can be frustrating—Facebook gets endless complaints every time they change the layout or add or adjust features. But it's a far more rapid and agile approach to development and deployment than shutting down the system while it is remade.

They are bilingual (if not multilingual): Kimberly Knight speaks two languages: the language of ancient practices and traditions and the online language of her virtual environment. But more than that, she understands the Christian heritage of her church and her congregation. She recognizes that there are patterns and symbols and rituals that hold deep meaning for people of faith and she has no interest in seeing them die off in the name of innovation. At the same time, she knows people of the Inventive Age have a different understanding and language than the

Christians who developed these symbols and rituals. So she is intentional about using them and translates when necessary.

Inventive Age leaders not only speak the languages of other times but of other places as well. The global understanding of the Inventive Age means that people are keenly aware that there is more than one expression of Christianity around the globe.

At Solomon's Porch, our people are always off to some far-away country. We have people building homes in Guatemala, working with women and girls who have been rescued from the sex trade in Thailand, training college students in Uganda, and building wells in India. They want an expression of faith they can take with them when they go, one that can absorb the changes they experience and carry them back to our community with new gifts for us.

This need to communicate in multiple settings will call for more understanding and more knowledge than ever. This interconnected knowledge requirement will demand new and more extensive training for leaders. Of course the people who need this training will also be the best suited to create it.

They make room: Pam pastors a church in a community made up of transplants from other parts of the country. Because they come from varying religious backgrounds, they often find themselves stuck in conversational confusion. She explains:

> In our church you find people who speak very differently about their experience with God. We have a couple that has been active in Baptist churches and non-denominational mega churches. They were having a conversation with a couple who moved

from New England after attending a mainline liberal protestant church. When the Baptist background folks described their conversion as "falling in love" with Jesus, the New Englanders were completely confounded by the description. They spoke of being "convicted" and "broken," which raised considerable confusion with this New England couple as well as some other members of the group. The mainliners struggled to understand how their commitment to a God that calls them to "social justice" and "being in relationship" with other people could also be described as "falling in love with Jesus." Ordinarily these two couples would attend churches that only spoke in their [respective languages]. But at Vision, one couple can be challenged to show its love for Jesus through social justice ministries and the other can be challenged to add emotion and compassion to its intellectual faith.

The church in the Inventive Age has to make room for people of vastly different backgrounds. We can't play favorites or, worse, make everyone who isn't us the bad guy.

They redefine "real": "I know Koinonia online sounds weird," says Kimberly Knight. "I hear it all the time. People tell me that it's not real church if it's not real brick and mortar. But my hunch is most Christians would agree that a building is not the church either. The community of believers is the real temple, the real church."

THIS AGE IS ABOUT COULDS.

The virtual nature of Kimberly's church is not all that different from the casual nature of a pub church or a coffee shop church. Most of us grew up with expectations about what church should look like. But the Inventive Age is not about shoulds.

It's about coulds.

What could the church look like? What could it feel like?
What could it be if we put our best efforts into creating
something beautiful and meaningful?

For people of the Inventive Age, finding the answers to
those questions is as real as it gets.

HEART

They are looking ahead: Every new age
faces the temptation to fix the problems
of the past. This is certainly true when it
comes to the church. When churches get
started, there's a tendency to be defined by what they
don't want to be: We don't want to be big. We don't want
to be "cheesy." We don't want to be closed-minded.

But the church of the Inventive Age is filled with far too
many opportunities and challenges to waste time trying to
right the wrongs of the past.

In the early days of Solomon's Porch, we were well aware
of the temptation to be the opposite of every church we'd
ever been involved in. So we made two rules:

> NO COMPLAINING ABOUT ANYTHING UNLESS
> YOU'RE WILLING TO MAKE IT BETTER.
>
> WE WILL BUILD ON THE POSITIVE EXPERIENCES
> FROM OUR PAST.

This commitment to finding the things that worked in our
lives to this point—and there many of them—kept us busy

for the first year. It soon became our habit to focus on what we could do and to hold on to the best of our past.

Don is the pastor of Vision Church in New York. He told me:

> Early on, in an effort to be creative or innovative, I would reject ideas if they rang too familiar. Sometimes it was something minor like wanting air pots for the coffee table—I didn't want the typical church fellowship hall coffee urns. Sometimes it was more significant issue, like me avoiding preaching on the Atonement for the first few years. I didn't want to preach about fountains filled with blood or penal substitution. Eventually, I learned there were other ways to speak about the Atonement and that something essential to the Christian narrative is lost when we avoid it. I also learned those coffee urns are the most efficient way to make coffee for 100 people. Turns out our predecessors in faith actually had some wisdom to share with us.

They curate the past: Leadership in the Inventive Age church will require the skills of a curator who cares for the artifacts of the previous ages. One of the myths about the Inventive Age is that it's all about the future. But people of the Inventive Age know that we bring the past with us. We want to honor the trajectory of history by building off of the best of what came before us and laying the groundwork for the inventiveness of future generations. Churches in the Inventive Age need leaders who can connect present-day expressions of faith to their roots in other times and other places.

They major in the minors: My friend Joel started an organization called ServLife. He seeks to create partnerships between people in developed countries and the those in developing countries.

This week I received a message from Joel:

> Hey Doug, we are seeking 20 younger Americans to start a conversation with us about giving 2 years of their life to go overseas and serve our 150 national church developers, child sponsorship, and micro-enterprise efforts. Could we have 5-10 minutes in one of your gatherings to see if any folks would like to join us? Not be promoting or fund-raising but only recruiters partners.

In our community, this kind of request is not a special announcement or an interruption in our schedule. It's the reason we gather. We want to be about what God is doing in the world and we never know what that's going to be. One week it's a South African pastor telling us about the AIDS orphans who need bikes. (We sent him home with enough money to buy a bunch of them.) Another week it's a guy from our church showing us slides from his trip to deliver aid supplies in Haiti. If the sermon gets shortened because of it, that's okay with us. In fact, it is often preferable.

They focus on meaning: This is where I fear for the church mentioned earlier that is the first on Facebook. A church must be meaningful to matter in the Inventive Age. It's not enough for it to be cool or casual or hip or funky. It has to have meaning. I'm not sure a church just using a Facebook group for their own promotion can pull that off.

The value of meaning isn't just about creating deeper spiritual experiences for the congregation. In fact, that's how many churches lost their sense of meaning for people in the Inventive Age. They became so focused on personal salvation, on getting to heaven, that for many Inventives the church lost a greater sense of purpose. They long for spiritual communities in which their faith matters—not only to them, but to the world around them.

Lori told me about Ordinary Collective, a ministry in Grand Rapids, Michigan. She wrote:

> Ordinary Collective is still in its infancy—perhaps even gestation—but what initially brought us together was the opportunity to explore the experience of the Divine in an artistic, communal, and generous way. Last fall, Grand Rapids was fortunate to host a citywide arts festival open to any artist entrant who could find a venue. Drawing together as a loose group of acquaintances, we contacted an arts-oriented drop-in facility for low-income neighbors. Together with this ministry, we collaborated on an interactive installation that explored both the presence and absence of God. No/W/Here, as we called it, hosted families, art aficionados, and homeless guests, side-by-side, inviting us all to simultaneously release our understandings of God and invite God's presence in new ways. Through this early joint project, we cemented a commitment to faith as an open-handed, communal process—one which is hospitable to all neighbors and which can be expressed in creative, interactive ways.

Ryan is part of an ecumenical team in Bellflower, California, that works for holistic community transformation. He says:

> Two years ago, Kingdom Causes Bellflower started Good Soil Industries, a landscaping business that holistically communicates the gospel to neighbors who are formerly homeless or those redeemed with rap sheets. Good Soil Industries provides discipleship and life skills training paired with a transitional job opportunity where that

training can be tried and proven. People who are underemployed and/or in rehabilitation will be empowered to obtain sustainable full-time employment and move closer to God. God's people have stepped up. Business people are sharing their expertise in marketing. Human resource professionals are helping to train people for interviews, and retirees share their experience and time riding along with the work crews for discipleship and quality control. It is a great example of God's people in a community united in God's kingdom mission.[1]

Both of these ministries create meaning—not just for the people involved, but for those who benefit from

THE CREATIVE IMPULSE OF THE INVENTIVE AGE IS STRONG.

their work as well.

They don't know who will show up: The changes of the Inventive Age are not reserved for one group of people. They are not the property of young people or white people or American people. The understanding and values and aesthetics and tools of the Inventive Age cross all demographic boundaries.

That's why one of the biggest mistakes a church in the Inventive Age can make is to assume it has a target audience.

Kimberly Knight, the pastor of Koinonia says:

The folks participating in online church are by no means exclusively kids, youth or twenty-some-things. The people who call Koinonia Congregational Church their spiritual home are young and old, black and white, American and European, gay and straight, and represent a spectrum of differently-abled bodies. One parishioner who has worshipped at Koinonia for nearly two years is a grandmother who lives alone and has experienced more than forty surgical procedures. Though home-bound, she finds solace in a living Christian community that daily prays with her, visits with her, and worries about her when she is not around. One young woman, a lesbian living in a small southern community, came to Koinonia with deep wounds inflicted by her home congregation. Finding a church in her hometown was hard. In our church, she has found love and acceptance. Here she has found a deep connection with God and peace with herself. In the earliest days of this church's formation, a 19-year-old woman found the community she needed when she was dislocated from her family of origin. She had relocated across the country with her fiancé who was now stationed in Iraq, and at Koinonia she made a new family. The space was virtual, but the community was real. As a community, we prayed and waited for the safe return of her beloved. When news of his return reached Koinonia, we cried. I cried real tears of joy for her joy.

GUT

They are organic: The creative impulse of the Inventive Age is strong and people of the Inventive Age expect to put our stamp on the spaces and places we gather. But you can't force creativity. It has to develop and emerge out of who you are, not who you think you should be.

From the color of the walls to the style of music to the
way you pray as a church, your aesthetics will reflect the
understanding and values of your community. So focus
on those. A pastor friend told me, "Over the years, I've
learned to put our disciple-forming mission first and let
the creativity flow organically from there. When we stay
true to our mission, something new just emerges naturally, since that's the kind of people we are."

They speak of their time and place: We create our own
music at Solomon's Porch. We believe we are called to
contribute to the beautiful tradition of church music that
has come before, so we have several songwriters who
express our collective experience through music.

Part of our value system to have creative expressions of
faith that speak to who we are and what our lives are like.
Our music is an aesthetic representation of that value.
Other Inventive Age churches co-opt popular music from
artists like U2 and Bob Dylan and Bruce Cockburn to bring
a familiar aesthetic to their worship settings. Inventive
Age churches are intentional about creating art and
music and spaces that feel familiar. Coffee shops and
pubs and warehouses and living rooms are the kinds of
places we have our most meaningful conversations
outside of church. It's only fitting that we bring our faith
to those spaces.

 HANDS

They use what they need: For all the ways
we are an Inventive Age church, Solomon's
Porch has a sad Web presence. Our website
is outdated, we don't really use it internally,
and getting it fixed has become one of those things we
mean to get to and just don't. It's irritating and creates
hassles for people who want to know more about us.

We are not a very Web-oriented community. Many of us are on Facebook and Twitter and a number of us have blogs, but we don't connect primarily through those media. We tend to get together a lot. We have meals and go to concerts and host art shows. For an Inventive Age church, we are awfully low-tech.

THE TOOLS OF THE INVENTIVE AGE ARE CHANGING ALL THE TIME.

The tools of the Inventive Age are changing all the time. There are all kinds of ways for churches to connect with people, to let people know who they are and what they're about. But if you're using the tools just to use them, they won't mean anything. Tools are a way to accomplish your dreams, a way to express your values and create an aesthetic. So use what you need and don't worry about the rest. If an overhead projector is the best way to display song lyrics, use it. If phone calls are the best way to communicate a need, use them. Do what works.

FOR

WITH

AS

TO DOs

TO DOs

TO DOs

FOR	WITH	AS
LEND EXPERTISE	WALK ALONGSIDE	WELCOME IN
CREATE SPACE	SET ASIDE AUTHENTICITY	BE GRACEFUL
BE AUTHENTIC	LEND RESOURCES	TELL STORIES
TELL STORIES OF "HOW IT WAS"	BE A LEARNER	TRANSLATE
LISTEN	CHANGE	DEMONSTRATE
TRUST	TRUST	TRUST
HAVE FAITH	SHARE HOPE	LOVE

CHAPTER 11
THIS IS NOT THE END OF
THE ROAD

IF JESUS IS THE LIGHT, THEN WE HAVE TWO
CHOICES IN THE SONGS WE WRITE: WE CAN
SING ABOUT THE LIGHT, OR WE CAN SING
ABOUT WHAT WE CAN SEE BECAUSE OF
THE LIGHT.

—T BONE BURNETT

The Inventive Age is not the end of the road. In fact, the road might be the wrong metaphor. Roads are designed to go from one location to another. Civil engineers have to know the starting location and the ending location to make plans. We don't have that luxury.

The Inventive Age is more like flight. There is a wide-open sky. And while that creates a kind of freedom, it also creates a new set of considerations. A pilot needs to consider wind speed, altitude, geese. The pilot can set the instruments and let the plane fly itself, but she can't fall asleep on the job. The endpoint is far away and there might be some turbulence along the way.

Being the church in the Inventive Age demands a flight plan that takes into account the variables and risks of the open sky.

The Inventive Age isn't perfect. There is much we know now that we didn't know before, but there is far more to learn. At the same time, we need to resist romanticizing the past. Life might have moved at a slower pace, but it certainly wasn't simpler. For the most part, human beings are far better off now than at any other time in history. We are healthier, live longer, and have resources and opportunities that even our grandparents couldn't have dreamed of.

That's why we have to be faithful to the call of Jesus, the call to be God's people in this time and place.

THIS AGE REQUIRES US TO BE FULLY ENGAGED WITH OUR FAITH TODAY.

We share the story of change with Abraham and Moses and the Prophets and the 1st-century church. We have to ask the same questions they did: What does it mean to follow God in our circumstances? How do we believe in the context of this culture? What is the good news for our people?

It is not enough to know about the faith of the 1st, 5th, 11th, 18th or 20th centuries. We are not called to live a faith of those times, but a faith of ours. Jesus told his disciples the kingdom of God was at hand. That means now. Here.

From the start of the Jesus story right through today, Christianity has been a story of the time always being right for believing and living out the life of God in our world. Being the church in the Inventive Age requires us to be open to the spirit of God conducting change in all areas of our systems and structures. It requires us to be fully engaged in our faith today.

And that just might mean inventing the future.

ENDNOTES

CHAPTER 2
WE DON'T KNOW WHERE WE'RE GOING

1.   There are people who make the case that churches ought to meet on Sunday mornings as a remembrance of Jesus' resurrection. Unless they are also willing to meet at sunrise, I'm not sure that argument holds up.

CHAPTER 4
TWEETS FROM SPACE MATTER

1.   Scott Simon, "Space Tourist Launches into Book," National Public Radio's *Weekend Edition Saturday*, March 6, 2010, http://www.npr.org/templates/story/story.php?storyId=124391836 (accessed March 23, 2010).

2.   XPLANE, et al., "Did You Know 4.0," *YouTube*, Fall 2009, http://www.youtube.com/watch?v=6ILQrUrEWe8 (accessed March 23, 2010).

3.   Jason Kincaid, "A Look at Facebook's Reach Worldwide," *TechCrunch*, August 27, 2009, http://techcrunch.com/2009/08/27/a-look-at-facebooks-reach-worldwide (accessed March 23, 2010).

CHAPTER 5
CULTURE HAS
NOTHING TO DO WITH THE BALLET

1.   Jonathan Watts, "Ancient tribal language becomes extinct as last speaker dies," *guardian.co.uk*, February 4, 2010, http://www .guardian.co.uk/world/2010/feb/04/ancient-language-extinct-speaker-dies (accessed March 23, 2010).

2.   Martha Woodroof, "Endangered Alaskan Language Goes Digital," National Public Radio's *All Things Considered*, May 23, 2007, http://www.npr.org/templates/story/story.php?storyId=10357963 (accessed March 23, 2010).

3,   Woodroof.

4.   Ted Striphas, *The Late Age of Print: Everyday Book Culture from Consumerism to Control* (Columbia University Press: New York, 2009), 27.

5.   This story is a perfect example of not knowing where I know something. I don't know if I read this, if someone told me about it, if I heard it on the radio, or if it was sent to me by a friend.

CHAPTER 10
BEING THE CHURCH *AS* THE INVENTIVE AGE

1.   You can check out the work of Good Soil at the Pheifers, "Good Soil 2009," *YouTube*, 2009, http://www.youtube.com/watch ?v=wY1dt0CWumc&feature=player_embedded (accessed March 2010).

About the Author

Doug Pagitt is the founder of Solomon's Porch, a holistic missional Christian community in Minneapolis, Minnesota, and one of the pioneering leaders of Emergent Village, a social network of Christians around the world. He is also cofounder of an event and social media company and author of a number of groundbreaking books: *A Christianity Worth Believing*, *Church Re-Imagined*, *Preaching Re-Imagined*, and *BodyPrayer*.

Doug can be reached at:

Twitter: Pagitt
www.DougPagitt.com
www.ChurchInTheInventiveAge.com
www.facebook.com/ChurchInTheInventiveAge

Look for other Doug Pagitt titles coming soon from sparkhouse press.